Fraud and Education

Fraud and Education

The Worm in the Apple

Harold J. Noah and Max A. Eckstein

ROWMAN & LITTLEFIELD PUBLISHERS, INC.
Lanham • Boulder • New York • Oxford

ROWMAN & LITTLEFIELD PUBLISHERS, INC.

Published in the United States of America
by Rowman & Littlefield Publishers, Inc.
4720 Boston Way, Lanham, Maryland 20706
www.rowmanlittlefield.com

12 Hid's Copse Road, Cumnor Hill, Oxford OX2 9JJ, England

British Cataloguing in Publication Information Available

Library of Congress Cataloging-in-Publication Data
Noah, Harold J.
    Fraud and education : the worm in the apple / Harold J. Noah and Max A. Eckstein
    p. cm.
    Includes bibliographical references and index.
    ISBN 0-7425-1031-X (alk. paper) — ISBN 0-7425-1032-8 (pbk. : alk. paper)
    1. Cheating (Education) 2. Education—Corrupt practices. I. Eckstein, Max A. II. Title.

LB3609 .N67 2001
371.5'8—dc21

00-045921

Printed in the United States of America

♾™ The paper used in this publication meets the minimum requirements of American National Standard for Information Sciences—Permanence of Paper for Printed Library Materials, ANSI/NISO Z39.48-1992.

Fraud: The quality or disposition of being deceitful; faithlessness, insincerity. Criminal deception; the using of false representations to obtain unjust advantage or to injure the rights or interests of another. An act or instance of deception, an artifice by which the right or interest of another is injured, a dishonest trick or stratagem. A method or means of defrauding or deceiving; a fraudulent contrivance; in mod. colloq. use, a spurious or deceptive thing, colloq. of a person: One who is not who he appears to be; an imposter, a humbug.

Contents

Preface

When we completed our study of examination systems in eight countries, *Secondary School Examinations: International Perspectives on Policies and Practices*[1], we decided to omit a section we had planned on the subject of examination security but to retain the material for possible future use. This was despite the fact that we had gathered a fair amount of information on the topic. In every country the organizations conducting public examinations spell out the regulations to insure the security of the test papers and answer sheets, and they specify the conditions for administering their exams. Virtually all of us have witnessed the application of these regulations and conditions: IDs are checked, candidates are placed far enough apart to make it difficult to overlook a neighbor's work, special booklets or forms are supplied for candidates' answers, the authorities specify what materials and instruments may and may not be brought into the exam room, the examiner opens sealed packages with the test papers and at the end of the session counts and seals them for dispatch to the exam authority. Trips to the bathroom are discouraged and often even supervised. An air of formality and authority hangs in the air.

The regulations typically describe what proctors should do if a candidate is caught or suspected of cheating and what the penalties might be. In some countries, these procedures are quite detailed, and we were impressed with the jury system in the French *baccalauréat* and with "due process" as outlined in the German rules concerning the *Abitur*.

As the 1990s advanced, we noted a growing concern that cheating in important examinations was becoming more frequent and even more sophisticated. Reports of serious cheating scandals and ingenious modes of cheating appeared with increasing frequency in the press, not just in the United States but in other countries, too. Of course, the number of candidates taking "high-stakes" exams for school graduation and for professional licensure was growing all the time, so even if the rate of cheating remained unchanged, there were more instances to report. But we suspected that a greater tendency to cheat might be appearing, generated partly by steadily increasing pressures to do well in such exams, as well as by rapidly improving methods of electronic communication.

Plagiarism represents another facet of cheating. Many students have never had formal instruction to advise them on the appropriate use of another author's work. Given a topic to write on, they turn easily to shoehorning into their own efforts verbatim text from encyclopedias and other authorities, often even without attribution. Or they "borrow" another student's paper and submit the text as their own. Or they simply purchase a ready-made paper. These are all time-honored practices. But the technological advances of the past decade have made it possible to do these things in ways that are much more economical of time and effort. The Internet and e-mail are now the tools of choice for the would-be plagiarist.

Technical developments in document reproduction have had a similar effect on the likelihood that an official document offered as proof of identity might be false. A large industry has grown up to supply the demand for false birth certificates, driver's licenses, social security IDs, and even passports. Educational and professional credentials represent similarly valuable items of personal property. In many countries they too are apparently being forged in larger numbers than before. Organizations offering "quickie," if worthless, credentials (degrees, certificates, testimonials)—the so-called diploma mills—have also profited mightily from the growth of the Internet and e-mail. Now it is only too easy for someone living in, say, Germany, and desiring to work in one of the Persian Gulf oil states to equip him- or herself with a fraudulent U.S. diploma, attesting to a high level of education and training. The implications for the continued integrity of education, vocational and professional training, and selection for employment are serious indeed.

Finally, we were impressed, negatively to be sure, with the volume of reports of fraud in scientific and medical research. Again, the desire for the prestige that comes from being first with a scientific discovery or a life-saving drug motivates much of this kind of fraud. But recent years have seen the addition of a largely new element—the prospect of monetary gain from patent licensing and the availability of venture capital investment funds.

Unfortunately, but perhaps inevitably, education can no longer be regarded simply as a Good Thing, free from society's standard faults and taints. The view of education as perhaps an impersonal, but always a positive, force for individual and societal advancement is now challenged from various angles. We are forced to acknowledge that its participants are open to temptations and subject to weaknesses similar to those of people in business, government, professional sport, and the law—to name only a few of those other occupations in which spectacular frauds occur with depressing frequency. While we did not (and do not) wish to overstate the case—most exam candidates in most countries do not cheat, most holders of credentials in most places have come by them honestly, and so on—there is evidence that even in the best run schools and school systems, and in the best regulated professions, dishonesty is present and can become a serious problem. Trust in the integrity of the educational process is eroded as teachers, principals, and administrators, pressured to produce good test results, resort to unethical conduct and as confidence in the authority of academic credentials is weakened by the proliferation of fake diplomas. No less damaging to the public's confidence are revelations from time to time that scholarly, scientific, and medical research may be tainted with misconduct, also as a result of commercial, self-serving pressures.

For this reason we believe that there is value in presenting a selection of the most representative recent instances of fraud, identifying some of the causative factors, and suggesting some possible approaches to controlling the growth of academic misconduct. Hence this book.

We want to acknowledge the assistance given by friends and colleagues who responded to our initial ideas and who continued to assist with comments on our work in progress. We also owe special thanks for the many helpful comments, ideas, and data supplied, in particular, by Professor Mark Bray of the University of Hong

Preface

Kong and by Professor Dr. Juan Manuel Moreno, Vice-Rector for International Relations, Universidad Nacional de Educacion a Distancia, Madrid, Spain. We alone are responsible for whatever errors of fact, interpretation, or judgment are to be found in the present work.

Most of all, we thank and salute our wives who continued to encourage us in our interests, even though they might well have thought that they were entitled to more attention once we had retired from our respective teaching positions.

NOTE

1. Max A. Eckstein and Harold J. Noah, *Secondary School Examinations: International Perspectives on Policies and Practices* (New Haven: Yale University Press, 1993).

Chapter 1

The Fraud Problem

"Cheating in Our Schools; A National Scandal," *Reader's Digest*, October 1995: 65–70.
"Settlement in NASDAQ Case. SEC Fines 28 Firms $26M; 51 Brokers Suspended," *Associated Press*, 11 January 1999, Internet.
"As College Costs Increase, Scholarship Fraud Follows," *New York Times*, 11 November 1998: A1, 22.
"Benefits Fraud Exposed," *The Times* (London), 5 February 1999, Internet.
"Easy Degrees Proliferate on the Web," *New York Times*, Education Life, 2 August 1998.
"Honors for Sale," *World Press Review*, May 1999, 46(5):39.
"Welcome to College. Now Meet Our Sponsor," *New York Times*, 17 August 1999.
"Olympic Scandal Spreads to Sydney, Second IOC Official Resigns," *Associated Press*, 22 January 1999.

CHICANERY IS EVERYWHERE

The ordinary citizen may be forgiven for believing that no area of human activity is exempt from fraud. After all, reports of fraud are published in the mass media only too frequently. Whether it is high finance or journalism, the art market or law enforcement, the practice of medicine or journalism, instances of fraudulent behavior abound.

One commentator, Russell Mokhiber of *The Corporate Crime Reporter*, has even published a list of 100 "Top Corporate Criminals of the Decade," available on the Internet. Each of the companies listed had been prosecuted, convicted, and fined for breaking U.S. laws. Predictably, Mokhiber describes his list as just the tip of a massive mountain of corporate fraud and criminality, ranging from breach of environmental, campaign finance, and food and drug regulations through antitrust violations, fraud, financial crimes, false statements, illegal exports, illegal boycott, worker death, bribery, obstruction of justice, public corruption, and tax evasion. Even if one discounts Mohkiber's indictment to compensate for his crusader's zeal, he provides solid justification for the common perception that corporate America is no stranger to serious misconduct and even downright criminality.

For example, in mid-1999 the newspapers revealed that Mr. Martin Frankel, fraudster extraordinaire, had apparently been bilking a slew of insurance companies to the tune of at least $200 million over the previous seven years. He promised the companies low brokerage fees on their bond transactions and high returns on their investments, both very attractive propositions. Instead, he squirreled away abroad much of the money entrusted to him, while living it up at home on the remainder. Only when state insurance agencies began pressing their questions too close for comfort did his fleecing of the insurance companies come to an end. Barely ahead of the investigators, Mr. Frankel absconded to Europe, where he enjoyed three months of liberty before being apprehended in Hamburg, Germany.

Also in 1999, in the world of high finance, A. R. Baron, a Wall Street firm specializing in penny stocks, was revealed to have defrauded its customers by trading on their accounts without their permission, in the process losing over $30 million for them. Bear Stearns, a leading Wall Street firm, was accused of knowingly abetting A. R. Baron in its fraudulent activities. Bear Stearns agreed to pay a settlement of $38.5 million to avoid court action. The ordinary citizen reading such stories gets the impression that at either extreme of the world of high finance, whether it is an individual con man like Mr. Frankel or a top-drawer firm like Bear Stearns, fraud and misconduct are an everyday affair.

The world of art dealing is a fertile ground for fraud. Here, if anywhere, the caution "caveat emptor" must be taken seriously, for forgeries of every kind of art object abound. Dealers and auction houses on the one side and customers on the other try to protect themselves by physical inspection of the item and, most importantly, by verification of its provenance. Faking provenances of forged paintings was the specialty of an Englishman, John Drewe. Drewe managed to pass off to dealers and auction houses about 200 forged pictures, supposedly painted by the likes of Braque, Dubuffet, Chagall, and Giacometti. Drewe's achievement was built on the most painstaking assembly of convincing documentation for the pieces he handled. He gained access to archives containing documentation about the painters and their work and actually altered the physical record to lay a convincing paper trail leading to the forged works he was hawking. According to one report of his career, "Drewe did more than slip phony pictures into a market hungry for important contemporary art—he altered art history."[1] Drewe now languishes in a British jail.

As in financial and corporate affairs, it is not only (or even importantly) isolated individuals who are tarnished by fraud in the world of art dealing. Blue-ribbon firms with international reputations have been implicated in some very questionable practices. Under a provocative headline, "Sotheby's Sold Fakes for Years," the *Sunday Times* (London) reported a number of instances in which professional and lay purchasers of "antique" furniture were, in fact, sold with faked items:

> The two most senior executives in the furniture department have already resigned after four "Georgian" chairs that sold for £1.3m [about $2 million] were exposed as forgeries. It has now emerged that two other wealthy clients have also bought "period" furniture at Sotheby's that was counterfeit. An "eighteenth-century" Carlton House desk sold for about £80,000, a pair of "Regency" torchères [tall stands for holding candelabra] for £44,000, and a pair of "George III" jardinières for £16,000 are among the bogus goods sold at auction to unsuspecting buyers in recent years.
>
> "The trade has been pointing out for years the suspicious items of furniture that have been turning up in Sotheby's," said Michael Hogg, a London antiques dealer. "Given the period of time and the number of suspect goods, I think the trade and the public have a right to know what was going on. They should now go back over every lot sold by any suspect sources, contact the purchasers and look at them again."
>
> Graham Child, who was a Sotheby's director and senior specialist, has admitted failing to spot the fake Georgian chairs but would not comment on other forgeries offered to buyers. "Who doesn't have some problems at some juncture?" said Child, fifty-two, who was

with the company for twenty-one years. "People can get things wrong. Nobody is as pure as the driven snow. I have left Sotheby's, I am carrying on my life and I would really rather not comment on what has gone on in the past."

Dealers claim that during the 1990s there has been a pattern of suspect items sold at Sotheby's that they believe originate from at least two sources. Bonhams, another London auctioneer, said it had raised concerns with Sotheby's two years ago involving one supplier. Several of London's most respected dealers have also complained to the company about the amount of suspect furniture sold in its New Bond Street saleroom.

The controversy over fake antiques at the world-famous auction house has flared up after the sale of two pairs of chairs said to come from St Giles's House in Wimborne, Dorset, the seat of the Earl of Shaftesbury. They are now known to be fakes and do not come from St Giles's House. The first pair was bought in 1994 for £463,500 [about $750,000] by Herbert Black, a Canadian scrap metal merchant millionaire. The second pair fetched a world-record price of £837,500 when it was sold two years later. Dealers were staggered that Sotheby's had failed to spot the fakes, with one expert claiming it was the "equivalent of the British Museum misreading the Elgin Marbles."[2]

Turning to one of the most sensitive areas of community life, we have a right to expect that those charged with enforcing laws will act uprightly themselves. Too often that expectation has been disappointed. In 1997 the U.S. Department of Justice reported a long string of sloppy and fraudulent practices in the FBI's famed crime labs, ranging from the employment of forensic scientists who lacked appropriate qualifications to the doctoring of lab reports. State and city police units in diverse locations of the United States have come under suspicion of planting false evidence in order to justify arrests and convictions and even of perpetrating summary executions. As we write, the Los Angeles Police Department is once again under a cloud, this time in connection with the actions of one of its specialized units, the so-called Ramparts Division. What began as a fairly routine arrest of one of the Ramparts officers for stealing cocaine from police evidence lockers turned into a major public scandal when the arrested officer gave evidence, in return for a reduced criminal charge, of widespread corruption and worse in the unit. He admitted shooting an unarmed citizen on the street and having his partner plant a rifle at the scene in order to substantiate a claim of self-defense. Meanwhile, inquiries have gone far beyond the Ramparts Division, with twenty-three convictions already overturned by February 2000, and more to come. The *Los Angeles Times* reported, "Investigation has uncovered evidence of unjustified shootings, beatings, drug dealing, false arrests, witness intimidation, perjury and planting of evidence. To date, 20 officers have resigned or been relieved of duty, suspended without pay or fired in connection with the scandal."[3]

None of this is new in the world of policing or, indeed, confined to the United States. Two high-profile cases in England cast the gravest doubt on the probity and professional competence of the police, forensic crime experts, and the system of court justice. The cases were quite similar and were popularly known as "the Maguire Seven" and "the Birmingham Six." They both concerned Irish immigrants to England accused, tried, and convicted of manufacturing bombs (the "Seven") or planting and exploding bombs (the "Six") on behalf of the Irish Republican Army. By 1991, when the British Court of Appeal eventually quashed all the verdicts, the accused had already served many years in prison—the "Six" had each served sixteen years, and one of the "Seven" had actually died in prison. After bitter and prolonged public campaigns demanding a review of the cases, it was established that the police had planted some evidence while suppressing other evidence. In addition, it was shown that the forensic scientists (whose testimony had been crucial for the state's case) had willfully suppressed evidence that would have raised doubts about the accused's guilt, as well as having been seriously professionally negligent. Nor did the British court system of justice come out unscathed from the scandal. The courts and especially the appeal judges were shown to have been excessively obstinate in their sustained denial that any injustices had been done and especially culpable in their reluctance to admit that the appearance of new evidence might warrant reopening the cases.

Journalism is yet another area of public responsibility to have recently provided examples of deliberate professional misconduct. The pressing deadlines characteristic of journalism compel editors to rely heavily on the integrity of their writers and reporters. From time to time their trust is betrayed. Thus, it was learned that between 1995 and 1998, Stephen Glass, a writer, made up part or all of forty-one of his articles for the *New Republic*. Then, only a little later in 1998, Patricia Smith, a prize-winning *Boston Globe* columnist, was fired from her job, accused of fabricating at least four of her columns. The same newspaper suffered a further blow to its reputation when in the same year another of its star columnists, Mike Barnicle, was found not only to have passed off fiction as fact in a number of his stories but also to have plagiarized some one-liner jokes for his column.

One could go on and on, through virtually every area of human activity—politics, organized religion, commerce, the legal profession, medicine, engineering, and governmental administration—not only in the United States but all over the world, citing instances of fraud, corruption, and professional misconduct that come to light daily.

FRAUD IN EDUCATION AND RESEARCH

While we are not inclined to think of serious misconduct in connection with education and research, fraud exists (some would say even flourishes) there, too, and is certainly not new. Nor is misconduct in education limited to any one country. Wherever there are exams, there is cheating. Wherever credentials are valued, there is fraud. From time to time, teachers, professors, and educational administrators abuse the trust placed in them, and researchers fabricate or "massage" their data and falsify their reports.

One of the earliest examples of an exam crib, on display in the Field Museum, Chicago, is a strip of silk fabric with 117 rows of notes written on it. This seventeenth-century artifact was probably used in the oldest national, public exam system in the world, that of Imperial China. The candidate would wind the silk round his arm so that it was available for surreptitious consultation during the examination. An even more elaborate device of the same genre is the "Cheating Shirt," which may be viewed on display in the Gest Library at Princeton University. This is an entire undergarment inscribed with texts on the Chinese classics. It is believed that a candidate for the imperial examinations used the shirt to cheat. For maximum security, candidates were required to write their exams in individual closed booths. Consequently, a candidate using the Cheating Shirt could remove his outer clothing and consult the reference material organized on his shirt. Although today's advances in technology enable exam cheaters to replace handwritten notes with electronic devices, the principle remains the same.

Two news items published in September 1998, on either side of the Atlantic, portray many of the elements of educational fraud we consider in this book. The first, from England, reports the dismissal from Oxford University of the Student Union president who was detected cheating on a final exam. She had obtained special permission to take her personal computer into the exam, alleging that she had hurt her wrist. Despite supervision by a special proctor, she was able to download a preprepared essay to hand in as one of her answers. Her injury was faked, and she was "sent down," that is, dismissed from the university, after admitting "unfair means" of taking the exam. What made this a newsworthy story was the fact that here was an apparently highly talented student, occupying an important elective office at one of the most prestigious academic institutions in the world, who nevertheless felt it necessary (or, at any rate, worthwhile) to cheat in her finals. She was not deterred by the risk of discovery or held back by the authority of the institution and its powerful ethic of scholarship and personal probity and responsibility.[4]

The other instance, not yet adjudicated, was reported on the front page of the *New York Times*. Cornell University officials had begun an inquiry into allegations of scientific misconduct against the director of one of its immunology research labs. Members of his team accused him of

> ordering subordinates to falsify data in one research grant application, of knowingly using false claims to obtain another federal grant for $1.5 million, of publishing a paper based on falsified experiments, and of threatening or punishing members of the lab who discovered damaging evidence.

Once again, the accused is a prominent member of a reputable academic institution. He had achieved recognition and success in becoming director of his laboratory and obtaining external funding for his research. Yet, if the charges are found to be true, he flouted the conventions, cast a shadow of doubt over his lab's research results, and risked his entire career and reputation.[5]

These are only two of the growing number of similar cases that have gained public attention in recent years. They may not be new to insiders in academia, but the general public tends, for the most part, to be unaware of both the nature and the extent of dishonesty in education, research, and training.

TYPES OF FRAUD

In this work we identify and analyze instances of fraud in education and research, treating it as a worldwide, and not just a U.S., phenomenon. We focus on three major aspects of such fraud: cheating by students, credentials fraud, and misconduct by professionals.

We deal primarily with cheating that has major implications beyond the classroom and the school: cheating in external exams, where the stakes are high and the results may have important and far-reaching significance, such as opening the door to higher levels of education and employment. Cheating in such exams makes use of many ingenious techniques. Even the following lengthy list covers only a fraction of the possibilities:

1. Two students sitting one desk apart share an eraser. The students write answers on the eraser and pass it back and forth.
2. Students write pertinent information on the visors of their caps, shirt cuffs, or the palms of their hands.
3. Students wear a 'walkman' portable radio with headphones which has recordings of pertinent information.
4. Students store answers on hand calculators, then use and/or share the calculators with other students.
5. Students arrange themselves at locations and angles so that they can easily pass information. Some of these arrangements include:
   a. the "power wedge" where students form a triangle with the knowledgeable student at the bottom point. Other participating students sit at higher levels, fanning out as the rows go upward;
   b. students sitting one seat apart but with pertinent books and papers placed on top of the separating desk;
   c. students sitting close enough to look at each other's exams.
6. Students use a code system such as tapping or hand signals to communicate back and forth.
7. "Ghost" persons, knowledgeable in the subject, take the exam by impersonating the real student.
8. Students appear to take the exam but do not turn one in. Later the students accuse the instructor of losing the exams and demand to be given a re-test or amenable [sic] grades.

9. One student creates a diversion by asking a question of the proctor so that the proctor cannot observe other students cheating.
10. Both a "ghost" person and the enrolled student take the exam. The "ghost" person puts the student's name on the exam and completes it. The student takes the exam but puts a fictitious name on it. Both exams are turned in. In the end, the instructor has no alternative but to discard the extra exam.
11. Two forms (A & B) of the exam are handed out. Students, who have gotten the answers to Form A prior to the test, may be given Form B. The students are instructed to code the answer sheet with whichever exam form they were given. These students code in Form "A" instead of "B" and then provide the answers they have previously gotten.[6]

When cheating on high-stakes exams occurs, whether by students or by teachers, there are potentially far-reaching consequences, not merely for the perpetrator but also for society at large. The implications extend beyond the individual and call into question the integrity of the exam system itself, the efficiency of the selection apparatus based on exam results, and the quality of the credentials of those who have passed the tests relying solely on their own honest efforts.

Cheating on exams is not the only type of misconduct in education. Plagiarism, passing off other people's work as one's own, is alive, well, and even flourishing in our schools, colleges, and universities. It extends from copying passages without proper attribution to blatant trading of commercially prepared essays over the Internet. Offers to ghostwrite academic papers and even dissertations are made using such euphemisms as "editorial assistance," "research assistance," "statistical consultation," and the like. Those who apply for such help are usually looking for something more than just "assistance"; and those supplying the service are well aware of this. Frequent advertisements in college newspapers and flyers posted on university notice boards make clear that the business of plagiarism and ghostwriting is booming.

Credentials fraud is similarly widespread. College admission officers in the United States are warned by their professional associations to be on the lookout for falsified transcripts—documents that have been altered or even completely manufactured. Agencies purporting to be colleges or universities advertise degrees virtually for sale. Academic credit is given for "life experience," "professional achievement," "hobby activities," and so forth. Requirements for study and learning are severely minimized or entirely absent. These diploma mills baldly announce their authority to award diplomas, some even claiming to be accredited by a public authority.

Moreover, the demand for false credentials appears to be on the increase, reflecting society's emphasis on the importance of possessing paper certificates. While many government agencies here and abroad are vigorous in their attempts to close down fraudulent credentialing outfits, others are less diligent. Loopholes abound. Suppressed in one state or country, diploma mills skip town or country to set up shop elsewhere. It is not uncommon for a company owning one of these "universities" to be legally incorporated in one state or country, issue advertising from another, and register degree candidates and collect fees in yet another. Improvements in telecommunications, in particular the advent of the Internet and e-mail, have given diploma mills a tremendous boost. You, too, can become a Doctor of Philosophy from the comfort of your home. The payment of a relatively small sum of money (maybe $3,000 or $4,000) will secure one's registration, together with a guarantee that there will be absolutely no inconvenient demands made on your time in the form of the need to study, do research, write reports, or defend your work. In a few weeks a handsome diploma attesting to your new academic credential will arrive in the mail, ready to frame or include in your curriculum vitae package.

Unfortunately, students are not the only ones who cheat; sad to say, professionals in education and research are from time to time involved. Compared with the ubiquity of student cheating, cheating by educational professionals is rare, but it, too, is a growing phenomenon. In many countries teachers are open to bribery by parents and students for good grades; in some countries it is virtually an expected and accepted practice. As far as outright bribery of school and college professionals is concerned, its occurrence in the United States is much, much less than that in present-day Russia, the former Soviet Union, or Nigeria, China, and Japan, for example. However, even in the United States, teachers, principals, and central office administrators have been implicated in cheating. The public and the politicians demand that students turn in good test scores. That pressure transmits itself to teachers and principals, with the result that some teachers succumb to the temptation to "improve" their students' answer papers before they are submitted for grading. Those with prior access to test papers (examiners, printers, delivery agents) have been known to leak or even sell copies. Even the tightest security arrangements can be, and sometimes are, breached.

Policies governing the operation of the school system can also motivate misconduct by professional personnel, exemplifying the operation of the law of unintended consequences. For example, school districts receive more funds the greater the number of special education children enrolled, a policy that seems sensible and attracts widespread support. But when principals assign students to special education programs because that is a way to beef up resources for their schools, they are committing more than just egregious fraud; they are jeopardizing the entire future of those students. Similarly, there are occasionally reports that students with poor academic records have been assigned to special education programs primarily to prevent their low test scores from dragging down school or district averages.[7]

Nor is scientific research exempt from instances of major misconduct, despite the aura of probity that surrounds science. Standards of proof may be demanding, and the requirement that results be replicable insisted on, but still fraud occurs. The instance cited above involving the director of a Cornell University medical research lab may be atypical, but it is by no means unique. Since about 1980, fears have been expressed that the distribution of electric power causes biological damage. Accusations were made that everything from high-voltage bulk power transmission lines to computer monitors and electric blankets produces electromagnetic radiation fields promoting cancer in human beings. In 1992, Dr. Robert P. Liburdy, working at the Lawrence Berkeley Laboratory in California, published two scientific research papers supporting a link between the radiation and calcium signaling within body cells. The papers garnered much attention as virtually the only scientifically demonstrated evidence of a causative link between such radiation and cancers in human beings, a score of other studies on the topic having failed to support the notion that there is such a link. Then in mid-1999 investigators at the federal government's Office of Research Integrity (ORI) concluded that Dr. Liburdy had faked his data to support his conclusions. While denying culpability, Dr. Liburdy nevertheless agreed to resign his position at the Berkeley lab and to withdraw his findings.[8]

Embarrassments of this kind are not rare. The pressure to secure funding, faculty positions, and lab space is real. Many researchers live from one grant to the next. Often they have to consider not only their own immediate prospects for continued work but also the future of their assistants. Above all, there is the desire to be first to publish significant results; in scientific research, being second doesn't count. There are thus many temptations to fudge findings, to dress them up to make them appear more certain and more important than they really are—even to fabricate data and results, as Dr. Liburdy is said to have done.

ORI is charged with investigating allegations of research misconduct involving the use of federal funds. In the first eight months of 1999 it issued nine notices of such misconduct by researchers (typically the misleading reporting or fabrication of research findings). The individuals named were working in a wide variety of institutions in many parts of the country: the Fox Chase Cancer Center, Institute for Cancer Research; the Laboratory of Membrane Biochemistry, New York Blood Center; Rush-Presbyterian-St. Luke's Medical Center; the Department of Infectious Diseases and Microbiology, Graduate School of Public Health, University of Pittsburgh; the Maryland Psychiatric Research Center, University of Maryland; the State University of New York at Stony Brook; and the Department of Molecular Physiology and Biophysics and Department of Cell Biology, Baylor College of Medicine—all well-respected research centers. Many other incidents of misconduct in scientific research are not reported to the ORI or, if reported, are not proven beyond doubt, so these nine cases are best regarded simply as tokens of the true severity of the problem.

Sometimes students are the victims of dishonest or dubious conduct. The scholarship scam is the most common fraud on students and their families. College-bound juniors and seniors are the targets for mailings offering privileged, "insider" access to scholarship funds or "special tuition discounts" at U.S. or foreign universities. Once the required registration fees for the "service" are paid, the student is unlikely to hear anything more. A public service organization, College Parents of America, in conjunction with the U.S. Federal Trade Commission, has issued the following notice to alert the unwary:

FTC Consumer Alert!
Ouch! Students Getting Stung Trying to Find $$$ for College
May 1999
Need money for college? Doesn't everybody? With tuition bills skyrocketing, and room and board going through the roof, students and their families are looking for creative ways to finance a college education. Unfortunately, in their efforts to pay the bills, many of them are falling prey to scholarship and financial aid scams.

According to the Federal Trade Commission, unscrupulous companies guarantee or promise scholarships, grants or fantastic financial aid packages. Many use high pressure sales pitches at seminars where you're required to pay immediately or risk losing out on the "opportunity."

Some unscrupulous companies guarantee that they can get scholarships on behalf of students or award them "scholarships" in exchange for an advance fee. Most offer a "money back guarantee"—but attach conditions that make it impossible to get the refund. Others provide nothing for the student's advance fee—not even a list of potential sources; still others tell students they've been selected as "finalists" for awards that require an up-front fee. Sometimes, these companies ask for a student's checking account to "confirm eligibility," then debit the account without the student's consent. Other companies quote only a relatively small "monthly" or "weekly" fee and then ask for authorization to debit your checking account—for an undetermined length of time.

The FTC cautions students to look and listen for these tell-tale lines:

"The scholarship is guaranteed or your money back."

"You can't get this information anywhere else."

"I just need your credit card or bank account number to hold this scholarship."

"We'll do all the work."

"The scholarship will cost some money."

"You've been selected" by a "national foundation" to receive a scholarship—or "You're a finalist" in a contest you never entered.

One close observer of these scams estimates that in the U.S. alone approximately $100 million a year is being extracted from the pockets of students and their families by these scholarship frauds.[9]

Students risk being victims in other ways, too. When instructors or educational administrators lack the qualifications they need to have to do their jobs properly, their students are the victims. In the United States it is entirely usual for school districts to require teachers to provide instruction in subjects in which they have had little or no academic training themselves. But when administrators put un- and underqualified teachers in front of their classrooms, students are being cheated in the most flagrant manner. Thus, in addition to all of the exam cheats, all of the plagiarists who steal and make use of the work of others, all of the fraudsters who purchase and make use of false credentials, and all of the researchers who falsify results, there are all of the educational professionals who follow policies and engage in practices that shortchange students and their families.

HOW DISHONEST?

In some of these respects the possibility of dishonesty is well understood. Teachers are usually alert to signs that cheating on tests may be taking place. Test agencies, such as the Educational Testing Service (ETS), issue elaborate guidelines about security procedures for use at test centers. Employers check the credentials of job applicants, perhaps not as often or as carefully as they should, but they are well aware of potential fraud. Editors check the facts of articles submitted for publication, again not always, as recent events at the *New Republic* and the *Boston Globe* demonstrated. And in science, results are not finally accepted until they have been independently replicated. But despite all the safeguards and attempts to detect and punish fraud, it is far from being eliminated.

Activities that are clearly criminal include stealing test papers, impersonating a candidate and taking a test in someone else's place, school principals "improving" students' answer sheets before submitting them for grading by the testing service, and using a false credential to secure a job or practice a profession. In the United States each state sets its own penalties for these infractions, as do foreign governments. Typically, punishments for isolated offenses are not severe. For example, in New York State impersonating an exam candidate is held to be a class A misdemeanor, which can draw a fine not exceeding $1,000 and/or a term of imprisonment from fifteen days to one year.[10] A first offence typically draws a reprimand and/or a small fine. Only in egregious cases, where a widespread conspiracy can be shown, will the law come down heavily on the offenders.

However, a practice need not be criminal in order for it to be dishonest. Selling or buying a term paper may not be criminal, but it is a commerce widely decried by educators. A teacher might use inside knowledge of questions on a test paper to coach his or her students; a job applicant might polish a resume by omitting the less flattering and exaggerating the more flattering features. In the business world, such activities would be described as "sharp practice."

Judgment in such cases is not always simple, if only because there may be conflict between important educational values. For example, teachers wish to see the work of a given pupil and not that of his or her helper, whether it be a fellow student, a parent, or an older brother or sister, so they tend to discourage students from copying their neighbors' work or whispering answers to test questions. But at the same time, they would like to encourage cooperation among the students, "helping each other," "working together." In some classes, for some activities, group projects may be arranged, and the same grade awarded to all members of a working group, regardless of individual contributions. In this way, ambiguous, even conflicting, messages are conveyed: It's OK to collaborate and piggyback on other people's work in some circumstances—but don't do it in other situations. To make the required discrimination is not easy, either for students or for teachers.

From one point of view a practice may not look particularly honest, but from another perhaps there is justification. When a senior professor places his or her name first on the list of authors on a research paper for which juniors have done all the work, is that as reprehensible as it looks at first glance? Or is it simply an appropriate acknowledgment not only that the professor has provided the lab space and other facilities for the work but also that the senior takes full responsibility for the integrity and accuracy of the work of his or her juniors? When colleges give admission preference to the children of alumni (and particularly to the children of alumni who are donors) is that an unfair practice, or is it just a decent recognition that a college is like a family, extending through time and over generations, recognizing important and valid ties of rights and obligations?

When a tutor or parent assists a student in preparing a research paper, where is the appropriate limit? What if the tutor identifies a bibliography of works the student should consult? Is that acceptable, whereas going to the library and searching out the books for the student is not? Or is that acceptable, whereas reading the sources and providing the student with summaries of the relevant content is not, and so on?

What attitude should we take to the commercial advertising and sponsorship now increasingly being introduced into classrooms? The trend accelerated sharply in 1989, when Channel One, a televised news and commentary service, was offered (together with television sets and satellite hookups) to schools in return for permitting a few minutes of commercials while the programs are aired during school time. Thousands of schools accepted the initial offer and continue to show Channel One's programs and commercials to their students. New York State is the only state to have imposed an outright prohibition on its public school systems against signing up for the service, viewing it as an unacceptable intrusion into the classroom. Yet, even in New York State, the state's public university system has taken advertisement time on Channel One to try to persuade more out-of-state high school students to consider coming to New York for their college education. Is it unambiguously fraudulent for state authorities to institute compulsory schooling and then to permit children's school time to be "wasted" looking at commercials? Or is that a reasonable tradeoff for exposing them to news material and commentary on serious public issues they might not otherwise encounter? There are persuasive educational and ethical points to be made on each side of the issue.

As troubling to some parents has been the appearance in school mathematics textbooks of exercises and examples containing direct references to (and illustrations of) products that appeal to school-age children: Nike athletic shoes, Gatorade drink, Barbie dolls, Sony Play Stations, McDonald's fast food, and the like. One such text is McGraw-Hill's *Mathematics: Applications and Connections.* The book was first published in 1995 and was updated in 1999. It is used in many states and is selling well. Although the companies whose products are identified apparently do not pay for the exposure they are getting, they are obviously not discouraging it either. Educators are caught once again between competing educational values. They want to catch the attention of students and motivate their learning. What better way than to latch onto the very products so many of them know about, already use, or would dearly like to possess? But shouldn't children have some space in their lives where they can escape society's pervasive commercialization?[11] When it comes to judging misconduct in education and research, gray areas abound.

Students may have little respect for the tasks their teachers set them or the rules their schools or colleges ask them to follow. They may feel they are being harassed with too much busy work or constrained by an oppressive list of dos and don'ts. This is the context in which cheating can flourish. Even the youngest children, faced with what they consider to be unfair and arbitrary rules, soon learn ways to get around the prohibitions:

> Once, Corsaro [William A. Corsaro, a professor of sociology at Indiana University] spent close to a year in a preschool where the children had been forbidden to bring their toys into the classroom. Before long, he noticed that they had found a way around the rule: the children were selecting the smallest of their toys—the boys chose Matchbox toy cars, for example, and the girls little plastic animals—and hiding them in their pockets. These were only preschoolers, but already they were organizing against the adult world, defining themselves as a group in opposition to their elders.[12]

INCIDENCE AND CAUSES

By its very nature, the extent of cheating and dishonesty is impossible to establish exactly. When school and college students in the United States and England are asked to report their own experiences with cheating, the results are by no means uniform. Some estimates go as high as 80 percent of students reporting cheating on one or more exams; other estimates are much lower, between 15 and 20 percent. But numerous examples from around the world leave no doubt that as education systems have expanded, growing in scope and complexity, fraud in education has become a global phenomenon. Increasing numbers of participants in exams and in educational activities of all kinds ensure this. Accompanying the growth in the number of students is the proliferation of credentials testifying to completion of stages of study and (perhaps) acquisition of certain knowledge and skills. The frontiers of the "credential society" are everywhere expanding. And, as we shall show, improvements in electronic communications and document reproduction have improved opportunities for fraud while lowering the costs in terms of time and money of committing it.

The extent of dishonesty is strongly influenced by at least five factors: pressures on the individual to succeed and the concomitant penalties for failure; the expected reward to be gained; the opportunities to be dishonest; the probability of getting away with it; and the nature of the context, that is, the social norms governing such behavior. For the last fifteen years or so, since the middle of the 1980s, the benefits of greater competition in the economic sphere have been trumpeted around the world as never before. The failure of socialism as a viable, long-lasting economic model has facilitated the triumph of an ethic of individual advantage. But it is not only business that has been transformed by this shift in emphasis; education also is being asked to accept that there are major advantages to be gained from adopting a competitive model of organization and practice. While business quite naturally reckons its bottom line in either net profit or market share, schooling has been forced to find its own bottom line in test scores and school and district rankings.

Test scores are being promoted as the ultimate index of "educational efficiency, effectiveness, and productivity." In England, schools across the country are ranked according to student performance on external exams—the so-called league tables. In the United States annual listings of "top schools" and "top colleges" are published. The result is to place novel pressure on every participant in education. Whether one is a student, a teacher, a school principal, a central office administrator, or a politician in charge of education policy and provision, one's degree of success is going to be measured by individual, institutional, and even national test scores. School systems in the United States are ending the practice of "social (grade) promotion." Students must now demonstrate that they have reached a satisfactory level in their present grades before they can move up next year. Teachers, schools, and school districts are told that they will be judged on how well their students do on standardized tests of school subject matter. Staffing levels and financial resources, even teachers' bonuses, may well be tied to the results. Schools that persistently fail to bring their students up to standard face being placed in receivership, their operation taken over by state authorities. Students' average scholastic achievement can now be compared across states in the United States, using the results of the National Assessment of Educational Progress. Thus, even state legislatures and state superintendents of education feel pressure to push up their states' scores. Moreover, at the national level, comparisons across countries are increasingly available, thanks to thirty years of work done by the International Association for the Evaluation of Educational Achievement, the parallel studies mounted by ETS, and those currently being proposed by the Organisation for Economic Cooperation and Development in Paris.

For the past two or three years, high school seniors applying to the twenty or so most prestigeful U.S. colleges have experienced exceptionally fierce competition for admission. As the value (even the necessity) of a degree from a "good" college has become more and more evident, and as the economy has boomed, making it easier for more parents than ever to finance the high cost of an Ivy League education for their sons or daughters, high school graduates who would previously have considered themselves to be shoo-ins for admission have been turned away from two, three, or four of their colleges of choice. Admissions officers themselves admit embarrassment that they are being forced to deny admission to many applicants who fit perfectly all their scholastic, extracurricular, personality, and background desiderata. Moreover, the only prospect in sight is that the number of fully qualified applicants will grow even larger during the opening years of the twenty-first century.[13]

The result of all this is a truly unprecedented build up of competitive pressures at every level of the educational enterprise. Whatever may be the advantages in terms of producing enhanced effort and achievement, one thing is certain: Incentives to cut corners, fudge results, and behave dishonestly and even criminally have been formidably strengthened. Perhaps one needs to look no further to explain why fraud in education is so prevalent today and why it takes so many forms.

Severity of punishments is probably less important in deterring fraud than the certainty of detection. Penalties for cheating vary enormously from institution to institution and from society to society, and there is no evidence that the most condign punishment is associated with the least misconduct. Cheaters and fraudsters are risk takers, so it is their estimate of the chances of getting caught that is central to their willingness to accept the risk. Although opportunities to cheat and use false credentials vary, human ingenuity being what it is, there are no limits to the imaginative devices and scams employed to get around strict controls.

Nevertheless, we should also recognize that there are other influences on the degree of fraud observed. Above all, social and cultural context is important in explaining the tolerance of cheating and other fraud in education. We should expect that the more fraud, deceit, trickery, and nonobservance of rules and regulations are condoned outside of education, the more likely misconduct of all kinds will occur within education. In the United States, business and financial fraud is on the rise. Investors' complaints to the Securities and Exchange Commission were up over 10 percent in 1998 compared with 1997. The Manhattan (New York) District Attorney is busier than ever with cases against alleged fraudsters in every type of business. These and similar reports from across the nation justify a sense that the propensity to act fraudulently has grown over recent years.

In this connection, what should one make of the 1999 award bestowed by the American Economic Association on a young Harvard University economist, Andrei Shleifer? The award was the John Bates Clark medal, given by the association to an economist under forty years of age whose work in economics is deemed to be of greatest distinction. Mr. Shleifer's academic work is arguably distinguished, but the association was apparently willing to overlook aspects of his earlier career. When Mr. Shleifer worked for Harvard University in Moscow on a U.S. government AID project to help reform and bolster Russia's financial system, credible allegations were made that he used information he had gained in the course of his Moscow duties to speculate in Russian investment projects. As a result of the allegations, AID canceled the contract it had with the Harvard Institute for International Development. The federal government recently sued Harvard for $120 million, claiming that Shleifer had abused his position in the Russia program for personal benefit. Only a few years ago, given such circumstances, it seems hardly likely that the American Economic Association would have seen fit to confer one of its most honored medals on a person carrying such a moral burden. Have a general decline in business ethics in the United States and a greater toleration for doubtful conduct in financial matters had their impact on judgments made in education and research, too?

Transparency International (TI), an organization based in Germany, issues annual rankings of countries listed by order of "perception of corruption" taking place within each country. The index covers mostly corruption in business dealings but includes some estimates of corrupt behavior on the part of politicians, civil servants, judges, and police officers. Of the eighty-five countries listed in the 1998 index, the ten with the lowest perception of corruption were (from less to more) Denmark, Finland, Sweden, New Zealand, Iceland, Canada, Singapore, the Netherlands, Norway, and Switzerland. The countries at the foot of the table in the "most corruption" position were (from less to more) Russia, Ecuador, Venezuela, Colombia, Indonesia, Nigeria, Tanzania, Honduras, Paraguay, and Cameroon. It is worth noting that there is broad inverse correlation between level of economic development and level of perceived business and governmental corruption.[14]

The chief methodologist of TI, Dr. Johann Graf Lambsdorff, reports "a high correlation" (0.88) between the assessment of corruption among politicians and that among administrators (judges, police officers, and public servants), "pointing to a high correlation between the two aspects of the corruption phenomenon. . . . There is no strong evidence that countries differ by the prevalence of the one type of corruption against the other."[15] We do not have, nor are we likely to have, any similar cross-national index of the perception of corruption in education and research, but it is not unreasonable to suppose that corruption there will be broadly correlated with corruption in business and governmental administration. At least as far as cheating on exams is concerned, we have observed that there are countries (and they are exclusively the less economically developed) that exhibit and tolerate quite remarkable degrees of misconduct by students, teachers, and examiners.[16] At the other end of the scale, there are many countries in Western Europe offering little evidence of corruption in education.

FINALLY

Why is fraud in education an important topic? For one thing, exam results and credentials serve as evidence, even guarantees, of competence. Those who complete their training and studies in a given field are assumed to be competent to enter a society's workforce and perform their responsibilities at given levels of effectiveness. A complex modern economy depends on such assurances. If they are false, all aspects of the functioning of a society suffer. Second, assessments of individual competence and certificates, diplomas, and institutional imprimaturs go beyond guarantees of individual competence. They serve, too, as guarantees of a working system of education and training. Diploma mills devalue the academic currency represented by credentials. In particular, they cast a shadow over the operation of many reputable institutions that offer alternatives to traditional ways of acquiring education, training, and academic degrees. Revelations of fraud erode confidence in the system and the trust upon which it rests.

We shall be surveying the field of dishonest practices in education and training, bearing in mind that a continuum of reprehensibility exists, stretching from the downright dishonest to the dubious and questionable. It includes actions that may under certain circumstances even be acceptable, depending on the context and the observer. We proceed by looking first at cheating on high-stakes, external exams, citing examples from around the world. Then we consider the subject of fraud associated with educational credentials. We continue with accounts of various malpractices by educational professionals and researchers, including plagiarism, dishonesty in research, and misrepresentation of research data and results. We conclude with a discussion of the problematics of dishonesty, what we might call the gray areas, and with some consideration of the importance of these behaviors and measures to limit them. What can be done, and what needs to be done? In a final note, we will present some thoughts on the need for action and the measures that may be taken to limit these behaviors.

Although we will be presenting numerous domestic and international instances of misconduct in education, this book is not intended as a rejection of the basic ways in which education and research are currently organized and practiced, any more than a discussion of weaknesses in the U.S. Post Office, Congress, the Immigration and Naturalization Service, or the medical profession signifies an intention to do away with them. Rather, our intention is to highlight malfunctions, in the knowledge that no institution is perfect and that all are improvable. Some policies in education and research encourage actors to act inappropriately, whether as students, teachers, administrators, parents, or employers. Attention should be paid to diminishing those incentives. Finally, we suggest a few strategies, both narrowly within education and more broadly policy oriented, that could help restrain the growth of misconduct.

NOTES

1. Peter Landesman, "A 20th Century Master Scam," *New York Times Magazine*, 18 July 1999: 32.

2. Jon Ungoed-Thomas and Christopher Owen, "Sotheby's Sold Fakes for Years," *Sunday Times* (London), 5 September 1999, Internet.

3. Matt Lait and Scott Glover, "LAPD Chief Calls for Dismissal of All Ramparts Cases," *Los Angeles Times*, 27 January 2000, Internet.

4. John Clare, "Student Chief Sent Down from Oxford for Cheating," *Telegraph* (London), 9 September 1998, Internet.

5. Nina Bernstein, "Charges of Research Fraud Arise at Cornell AIDS Lab," *New York Times*, 26 September 1998: A1, B6.

6. "Practical Approaches to Dealing with Cheating on Exams," Illini Instructor Series, No. 4, Instruction and Management Services, University of Illinois at Urbana-Champaign, 1987.

7. See, for example, reports in California. See Richard Lee Colvin and Duke Helfand, "Special Education a Failure on Many Fronts," *Los Angeles Times*, 12 December 1999, Internet.

8. *Federal Register*, 17 June 1999.

9. Mark Kantrowitz, http://www.finaid.org, 14 June 1999, Internet.

10. New York State Consolidated Laws, chs. 55 and 80.

11. Constance L. Hays, "Math Textbook Salted with Brand Names Raises New Alarm," *New York Times*, 21 March 1999, Internet.

12. Malcolm Gladwell, "Do Parents Matter?" *New Yorker*, 17 August 1998: 53–64.

13. Ethan Bronner, "For '99 College Applicants, Stiffest Competition Ever," *New York Times*, 12 June 1999: A1, A22.

14. Transparency International and Johann Graf Lambsdorff, "The Transparency International 1988 Corruption Perceptions Index," Appendix A, Internet.

15. Johann Graf Lambsdorff, "Transparency International 1988 Corruption Perceptions Index: Framework Document," 14 September 1998: 5, Internet.

16. For a detailed examination of tricks and scams in the less developed countries, see Vincent Greaney and Thomas Kellaghan, "The Integrity of Public Examinations in Developing Countries," in H. Goldstein and T. Lewis, eds., *Assessment: Problems, Developments and Statistical Issues* (New York: John Wiley and Sons, 1996), 167–88.

Chapter 2

The Cheating Game

Cheat: To defraud; to deprive of by deceit. To deceive, impose upon, trick. To deal fraudulently, practice deceit.

Cheating on important exams occurs in every country of the world. Pay a visit to any room where an externally organized high-stakes exam is under way and you will see candidates bent over their desks, hard at work, concentrating on the paper in front of them, striving to recall the material of the subject and organize it as best they can in their answers. They are doing what they are supposed to do. But in every hundred candidates there may well be one or two who are not playing strictly by the rules. Another one or two may not even be the candidates they are supposed to be. These few are the cheaters, the impersonators, and the fraudsters.

Maurice Bowra, distinguished Oxford don, tells the story of a determined fraudster:

Among the candidates [for the Mods examinations at Oxford in 1927] was a man from Jesus [College] whom we will call Jones. His papers were remarkably good, and he got such high marks that we awarded him an undisputed first class. Genner [his tutor] displayed becoming modesty about having taught him so well, but gave no hint that he did not think very highly of him. Later, after the list had been published, a man wrote from Brighton to say that on looking at the composition papers set in the recent Mods he saw that they were the same as had been sent him before the examination by a Mr. Jones from Jesus and that he had on request written versions of them. Slowly the whole story came to light. Jones had stolen a complete set of proofs of the papers from Genner's room, copied out those which concerned him, and then returned the originals. The compositions were done for him by the man at Brighton, but the other papers, such as the unseen translations and the prepared books, he wrote out himself with the aid of dictionaries, cribs, and every other kind of aid. He took them with him into the examination room, and at the end of each period handed in the appropriate paper. Once he seems to have felt that had gone wrong, and he tried a different plan. He removed a pile of scripts, including his own, from the room of the examiner, took out his own and substituted a new one for it, and returned the whole lot when the examiner was not in. The examiner noticed that some scripts were missing, but when he came to correct them, found them all there, and assumed he had made a silly mistake. This explained why in his prepared books Jones was very knowledgeable about quite small points which he seemed to have memorized verbatim from such editors as Jebb. We thought he must have a photographic memory, but he had simply copied out the passages with very few changes. The matter went to the Proctors, who looked very carefully into it and proved that Jones had cheated on a colossal scale. His name was erased from the class-list, and he was expelled from the University. I am ashamed to say that my other colleagues and I were secretly not displeased that Genner had been shown up not only as grossly careless in his treatment of examination papers, which should be kept locked up, but in his smug acceptance of Jones as a good scholar, when he must have known that he was not. Jones made a noble attempt the following October to come up to Exeter [College] as his own brother, but his scheme was unmasked, and he was not accepted.[1]

Ethical conduct may not have been Jones's strongest point, but there can be no doubt he deserved an A for Effort, if only for Effort in Cheating.

The events in Bowra's anecdote occurred many decades ago, but dedication to the task of exam cheating seems to arise ever fresh in each new generation of students. Do-it-yourself instructions for making an ingenious low-tech piece of hardware recently appeared on the Internet and serve well to illustrate the genre:

> Here's what you'll need. A clear Evian bottle or any other clear drinking water in a plastic bottle of your choice. I find Dannon or Evian bottles to work the best though. . . .
> Ok here is what you do: Slowly and patiently peel the label off of the bottle but not all the way, leave enough of it on so you don't have

to worry about it falling off of the bottle. Next, go to a computer and print out exactly what you need to know on a cheat sheet. Don't get too greedy, write down just the basics of what you will need, you can edit this stuff later. Then, highlight all of your text then click on the font size and use 4. This will shrink the text super small. Then you print it out, cut it, and paste it to the inside of the label.

Make sure everything lines up right so it's not suspicious. It might look a little too small to read after you print it out but once you fill the bottle with water it will magnify the text and you'll be able to read it clear as day.

Either set the bottle on your desk or just take swigs of it when you need an answer. It works great and hasn't failed me yet![2]

The author of these instructions is no doubt imbued with serious dedication to his or her task. In contrast, some cheating probably occurs just for the hell of it. Youngsters may think of it as a cool lark, a test of their ingenuity, even a way to get back at "the system"—whatever the despised "system" may be. But most cheating occurs for solidly substantial reasons: competitive pressures, inability to cope honestly with the academic workload, the sense that "everybody does it, so why not me too?" and even perhaps sheer ignorance of or indifference to what constitutes unacceptable behavior. Good exam results make a substantial contribution to future life chances. But good results typically require prior study and learning. So when the stakes are high, some candidates, aided and abetted perhaps by their friends and families, are willing to go beyond the limits of fair and even legal competition. In consequence, cheating, impersonation, theft, and the sale and purchase of test papers are not at all rare in the world of exams.

By high-stakes exams we do not mean run-of-the-mill classroom quizzes or in-school exams but, rather, external exams such as the Scholastic Achievement Test (SAT) and Advanced Placement Tests offered by the Educational Testing Service (ETS) of Princeton, New Jersey, the American College Test offered by the American College Testing Program of Iowa City, Iowa, and such state-organized high school graduation exams as the New York State Regents exams. Scores on these exams can play a determining role in high school graduation and college entrance, particularly admission to highly selective institutions. In other countries, exams at a similar stage of the education ladder are likely to be even more critical than those in the United States, offering exceptionally significant rewards to successful candidates. These include, for example, the French *bac-calauréat*, the German *Abitur*, the Advanced Level of the General Certificate of Education in England and Wales, and the college entrance exams in China and Japan.

Nor are school-related exams the only high-stakes exams to be considered. Even higher stakes may well be attached to exams guarding the admission gates to commercial employment, professional licensure, civil service positions, military training and promotion, or U.S. citizenship.

The extent of fraud and misconduct in school, college, and professional exams is impossible to quantify exactly, but surveys of high school and college students in the United States and elsewhere are unanimous in reporting very high percentages of respondents admitting to some form of cheating on at least one important exam. Thirty, 40, even 80 percent of students in some surveys report that they themselves cheated at some time in their school or college careers.

In 1990, a questionnaire returned by 232 students at Rutgers University in New Jersey had only 22 percent reporting that they had never cheated in college, 45 percent saying that they had cheated in "one or two" courses, and 33 percent admitting that they had cheated so far in an average of eight courses.[3] Two years later in Massachusetts another study gave support to these rather depressing figures: 81 percent of the students responding reported that they had cheated during their college years.[4] In 1993, the U.S. Department of Education reported that three studies showed that between 60 and 75 percent of college students cheat.[5]

In 1996, Professor Donald L. McCabe at Rutgers University, who has done much significant work on student cheating in the United States, reported that overall cheating had increased only modestly (no doubt it is difficult to improve on estimates of 81 percent!), but he pointed out that technology-related cheating as well as cheating by women and ever more blatantly overt cheating were becoming more common.[6] Another study published in 1996 compared the incidence of cheating in college in 1984 with 1994 and concluded that cheating had certainly increased over the ten year interval.[7]

Cheating by secondary school students, whether on in-school assignments and tests or on external exams such as the SAT, occurs more often than the general public cares to know. In 1998, the Josephson Institute of Ethics surveyed over 20,000 middle and high school students across the United States and reported that 70 percent of high school students and 54 percent of middle schoolers admitted that they had cheated on an exam in the last twelve months. Also in 1998, the results of a poll of over 3,000 high-achieving sixteen to eighteen year olds (students with A or B averages, who planned to attend college after graduation) showed the following:

- 80 percent of the country's best students cheated to get to the tops of their classes;
- more than half the students surveyed said that they did not think cheating was a big deal;
- 95 percent of cheaters said they were not caught;
- 40 percent cheated on a quiz or a test;
- 67 percent copied someone else's homework.[8]

As far as high-stakes exams are concerned, ETS claims that of the two million or so entries each year on the SAT, fewer than two in 1,000 are ever questioned for irregularity. While ETS has not suffered from any large-scale cheating scandal in the administration of the SAT, high school students, when questioned, point to many opportunities for minor cheating and to specific occasions when they themselves cheated.

SAT candidates are provided with one booklet covering both the language and the math sections. Having completed one section, candidates are given a break during which they can mingle in the halls. Some will have completed the math section, some the language. Friends can exchange notes on what questions have come up and what may come up. Although candidates are expressly forbidden to go back over their first sections to amend answers, some students will do so. If the exam hall is not adequately monitored (as is apparently often the case), such infringements of the rules are to be expected. David Owen, in a scathing exposé of the SAT, presents numerous examples of poor oversight and sloppy proctoring.[9] But few in the exam and testing business would welcome turning exams into rigorously monitored experiences, if only because excessive control would penalize the majority of honest students.[10]

Although the company's administration of the widely used SAT I and SAT II on behalf of the College Board has not been marred by major cheating episodes, its handling of some of its other testing programs involving mainly older persons has been riddled with fraud and abuse, according to documents and interviews.[11] ETS has been criticized in the press for being less than candid about episodes of cheating on, for example, teacher licensing tests and tests given to would-be immigrants on behalf of the U.S. Immigration and Naturalization Service.

For $10 students intent on cheating can purchase a guide entitled *Cheating 101*.[12] The book describes the best methods of cheating in high school and college and somewhat disingenuously claims that it helps students guard themselves against becoming the "victims" of cheaters. The book has been banned at the University of Maryland and at Ohio State University, among others. While cheaters continue to use tried and trusted, basically simple, ways to cheat, techniques of cheating on exams are currently exhibiting brisk rates of "improvement" and growing sophistication. The availability and relative cheapness of miniature electronic and infrared transmitters, receivers, cameras, and computer keystroke recorders have enabled would-be cheaters to bring high-tech to the exam hall.

Much criticism of contemporary exam systems focuses on the inappropriateness of evaluating a semester's worth (or even a year or more) of teaching, study, and learning by administering just one or two exams. Increasingly, educational authorities are supplementing bare exam results with evidence from coursework, all of which is allied to the movement to supplant one-shot assessment of student achievement with so-called continuous assessment. Doubtless, such reforms make good sense, but there is a downside. It becomes a good deal more difficult to guarantee that the candidate's work is solely his or her own, done without benefit of help from parents, friends, classmates, or, ever more likely nowadays, the Internet. As far as the latter is concerned, there now exist numerous World Wide Web sites offering ready-made essays and papers on a multitude of topics. One very popular site is called the Evil House of Cheat. It provides off-the-shelf essays with content and format targeted at specified educational levels (high school, junior college, freshman year, senior year, and so forth) at different prices. In mid-1998 the site offered a set of sample essays on Galileo's life and work and historical and literary topics that could be perused without charge. Students were invited to submit specific requests by e-mail.

Another source of college course papers, Academic Term Papers, advertises itself on the World Wide Web as offering "THE

WEB'S LARGEST SELECTION OF RESEARCH PAPERS—OVER 30,000 ON FILE—AT THE LOWEST RATES." Twenty-five areas of study are listed, from anthropology to women's studies. Reports cost $7 per page, with a maximum charge of $120. They are supplied in double-spaced format on regular typing paper, "with footnotes and bibliographies included free of charge." Delivery is typically by e-mail, but fax, Federal Express, and regular mail are also offered, all with same-day shipping. Academic Term Papers will also fulfill special requests. One is left to speculate how many of the firm's clients will obey the injunction in the advertisement: "[These papers] are sold for research and reference purposes only and may not be submitted either in whole or in part for academic credit."

To some extent, purchasing term papers on the Internet is merely a substitute for the direct, face-to-face transactions that have presumably been going on since colleges and universities began. However, all indications are that the volume of dubious papers submitted has greatly increased and continues to increase. Nor should we expect anything different, in view of the vast growth in the stock of papers, the much greater accessibility to knowledge about that stock, and the substantial lowering of transaction costs involved in acquiring a ready-made paper.

Penalties for cheating range from the most lenient to the most draconian, but no evidence exists showing that harsh penalties alone reduce the amount of cheating. The carrot may work better than the stick: The University of Maryland has tried to stem the practice by arranging for students who promise not to cheat to receive discounts of between 10 and 25 percent on purchases at ten stores near the campus.[13] Individual cheaters pay a price for their cheating: loss of the feeling of satisfaction that exam success has been earned through one's own honest efforts, the mental and emotional strain associated with the fear of being caught, and the penalties and loss of face if one is actually caught. The social significance of cheating is also serious. A high incidence of cheating can be regarded as a rough indicator of low moral and ethical standards among the young population. Moreover, the social costs of cheating may accumulate. If it is thought to be common, public confidence in the fairness of exams as selection devices is undermined, as well as the value of exams as credible measures of achievement.

CHEATING AT HOME AND ABROAD

"Research and reference aids" like those just noted are not limited to users in the United States. In England, teachers and instructors are also concerned about the availability of material processed and ready for the plagiarist's use:

> Banks of essays on just about any subject are available on the Internet; you just have to know where to look. . . . [M]id-coursework essays of a typical length of around 3,000 words are readily available from unscrupulous companies looking to cash in on gullible students. . . . [S]tudents throughout the country are buying essays off the Internet, for about £50 [$80] for 3,000 words.[14]

Nor is it always necessary to pay for copying another author's essays and coursework: Dorian Berger, a student at Harvard University, maintained a website where anyone interested could find, read, and copy his A-grade papers. Available free of charge were essays with titles such as "The Goals and Failures of the First and Second Reconstruction" and "The Role of the Japanese Emperor in the Meiji Restoration."

In many countries, external exams are generally conducted under tight security, but security measures cannot be, and are not, 100 percent effective. Indeed, in some countries cheating during even the most important external exams appears to be almost the norm.

Some forms of cheating on exams are common and familiar. They occur wherever exams are given. At the simplest level are the obvious tactics—copying from another's answer paper, whispering questions or answers to a neighbor, or taking crib sheets into the exam hall. Certainly in these days of ready availability of devices incorporating quite sophisticated electronic technology, notes on shirt cuffs seem primitive. Ingenious variations on simple signals abound. Arranging different colored candies on the desk to communicate correct answers is one example. Another method reportedly used in China involves signaling answers on multiple choice exams by supporting the head with the left hand for A, wiping the forehead with the left hand for B, placing the right hand on the head for C, and wiping the forehead with the right hand for D.

We are now in an age when a mass of information can be smuggled into exam halls hidden in miniature computers disguised as watches or calculators. One report of high-tech cheating concerns private soldiers in the Thailand army sitting an exam at a university campus for promotion to noncommissioned rank. Candidates, who paid $1,500 to $2,000 for the service, secreted radio-controlled receivers and batteries in their underpants and activated transmission of the correct answers by appearing to scratch their groins.[15]

In England during the summer 1995 A-level exam season, an episode dubbed by the press "My Magic Calculator" threw the examining authorities into a panic. In the exams for some subjects, calculators are expected and even required. However, advanced models allow candidates to transmit and receive messages conveyed by infrared signals to other similarly equipped calculators in the exam hall and even outside. Apparently, these were in use by enterprising students until the middle of the exam season, when a perceptive proctor realized what was happening. The exam boards sensed a public relations nightmare and sent out emergency instructions to check all calculators. As a result the offending models were officially banned, but those who had used them before the ban were not penalized. Meanwhile, sales of infrared-equipped calculators doubled.[16]

By 1999 the TI-83 graphing calculator, a $100 device, was being used by students in most high school math classes. They are essentially handheld computers, equipped with the ability to be programmed and a sizeable memory. Their distinct upside for education is that they allow students to concentrate on mathematical reasoning, relegating the labor of repetitive computation to the calculator. Their downside is that the information and programs stored in them can be used to cheat on exams. Teachers and exam authorities are reluctant to ban them from exam situations because many subjects require the use of calculators as a normal matter. The result is that teachers have to check that the devices are cleared of extraneous information and programs before students can use them during exams.[17]

John Croucher, author of *Exam Scams*,[18] who teaches at Macquarie University in Australia, believes that cheating in exams has become epidemic and that a clampdown is needed on the use of all kinds of technological aids to cheating, including radio transmitters concealed in pens, satellite-connected pagers providing information from outside the exam hall directly to the candidate's desk, and mobile phones used in lavatories for the same purpose—as well as preprogrammed calculators.

Underlining Croucher's fears is the report from Edinburgh University, Scotland, that about sixty students, constituting half the class in computer science, used the university's internal e-mail system to exchange ideas and actual text for their submissions for course assignments. The students will be required to take and pass a special exam before being permitted to advance to the next year of their program, and they may face punishment, ranging from fines to expulsion. The irony is that while technology facilitated the students' cheating, it was also technology that confirmed what they had been doing. The university used computer software that identifies the probability of plagiarism by comparing sentence structure, syntax, word choices, and the like.[19] Furthermore, "new guidelines for staff produced by Strathclyde University [Scotland] warn that 'opportunities for doubtful or dishonest behaviour in submitting assignments for assessment are undoubtedly increasing.'"[20] In response, many universities in Britain are turning to computer-assisted means to check on possible inappropriate use by students of "ready-to-use" Internet-based material.

In Britain, public exams have long been relied on as entrance gates to the university and to civil service employment. Recent self-studies by the boards that control the system reported that fraud and cheating in public exams at the end of secondary school were not very widespread. In 1990, the Welsh Joint Examination Committee reported only nine cases of cheating among 243,217 subject entries in the General Certificate of Secondary Education (GCSE) exams (the candidates are mostly fifteen and sixteen year olds taking their first external public exam). Similarly, the Northern Examining Association found fewer than 100 cases of malpractice among 491,864 GCSE subject entries. As for the Advanced Level of the General Certificate of Education, taken by eighteen year olds who seek university admission, the Welsh board found no more than three cases of cheating in over 25,000 A-level subject entries. Moreover, the Schools Examination and Assessment Council, the agency that formerly supervised all the exam boards, thought it unnecessary to do any research on security and cheating.

The paradox, however, is that these highly encouraging reports are at odds with a survey of 1,000 second-year university students, released in March 1994, that found that cheating was rife. Thirteen percent claimed that they had copied a neighbor's work in some type of exam.[21] Thus, even in Britain, where public confidence in institutional probity has for long been generally high, suspicion of misconduct and doubts about the integrity of the system have grown.

Nor is the evidence coming from Australia encouraging. A survey of 700 secondary school students in one state reported that 70 percent of the respondents (all at private or church-related schools) admitted to some degree of cheating (typically, copying material from other students' work or from a book or changing answers on a self-scored test).[22]

In the former Soviet Union, the habit of students giving their teachers and college instructors presents easily slipped over into outright bribery for favors:

> "Why so happy?" I asked [the freshmen medical students].
> "The whole group went to the movies instead of taking a test. . . . [W]e passed the test, the whole group did."
> "Where, in the cinema?"
> "No, we simply bribed the professor. . . ."
> "And he paid us back by giving the test credit to all of us. . . ."
> "Not even bothering to ask a single question. . . ."
> They launched into their story. . . . The professor of Marxist philosophy was an inveterate alcoholic. . . . The freshmen were advised to bribe the professor with a bottle of brandy. . . . In exchange for the bottle, the professor had given credits to all students without asking them any questions. . . . When the professor entered to conduct the test, . . . the students solemnly presented him with the bottle, saying it was an advance gift for the Soviet Army Day. The alcoholic pounced on the bottle and darted out of the room, telling the students to wait for him. A few minutes later he returned, reeking of brandy. . . . [H]e simply put "credit" against each student's name in his log, whereupon the group was free to go to the movies.
> . . . [T]he students kept telling me one story after another: who of the professors was on the take and how much a credit at a test or a good grade at an oral exam was worth. As it happened, an average test cost 50 rubles, while a final exam was a more expensive item, costing as much as 150 rubles. The kids . . . wangled bribe money out of their parents; some gave readily, others grumbled at the expense. . . .
> . . . [W]hen they left, . . . I was thinking of the kind of society I had to live in: professors extorting bribes from their medical students; parents allotting graft money; everybody knowing about it and not giving a shit.[23]

As elsewhere, when students in contemporary Russia continue to cheat, they justify their behavior on the ground that the educational system and many of its personnel are themselves corrupt. A study of their attitudes has suggested that the turmoil in Russian society resulting from the breakup of the Soviet Union contributed to an already well established culture of dishonesty and misconduct in education and society.[24] Apparently, Russian immigrant students in New York City have brought with them homeland practices. A magazine report in 1995 charges that Russian students at New York City colleges routinely cheated in exams and on coursework.[25]

In one of H. R. F. Keating's mystery stories, set in India and featuring Inspector Ghote, the lovable detective is charged with investigating the theft and sale of exam papers. His superior officer briefs him on a new case: "In Delhi itself last year, 3,400 cheats in exams were reported. In Kanpur, I think it was, they had three rooms for their BSc exam, one at Rupees 1,000 where you could cheat on your own, one at Rupees 2,000 where you could take the help of the invigilators themselves and a Rupees 5,000 room where you could call for answers from outside."[26] In 1989, thousands of Indian students trying to enter American colleges were required to retake English Language Proficiency and other necessary tests because copies were widely sold in their own country beforehand.[27] In March 1996, in Kanpur (again, Kanpur!) all school final exams had to be taken barefoot to discourage students from carrying notes in their shoes. In Kashmir, militant Muslims and Indian officials are not accustomed to agreeing on very much. But one of the things they do agree on is the necessity to put an end to rampant cheating in exams.[28]

Indeed, in what has been described as the casual and cutthroat world of Indian higher education, today's students appear to claim the right to cheat, "as a necessary and even commendable ruse." In the Indian state of Uttar Pradesh, where cheating appears to be almost de rigueur, "a thriving, mafia-based industry specializes in leaking exam papers, forging mark sheets, and threatening invigilators with violence." An attempt in 1992 to deal with the problem by introducing new legislation resulted in hundreds of students being jailed. But the laws against cheating were too rigorously applied for the Indian situation: within twenty minutes of the opposition party coming to power in the state in 1993, the laws were repealed. In 1998, with the Bharatiya Janata Party now in power, an "Anti-Copying Ordinance" once again met with furious opposition, with the students claiming that it criminalized the education system: "The new ordinance provides stiff penalties of up to five years for anyone using violence while copying. . . . Normal business in both houses of the State Assembly was disrupted . . . when opposition parties demanded withdrawal of the legislation."[29]

None of this is new on the Indian subcontinent. In 1988, in neighboring Bangladesh, students were adamant about their "right" to receive help from outside the exam hall during national placement exams. When challenged, they went on a rampage in which more than 500 people were injured.[30] According to education officials in Bangladesh, nearly 11,000 students were expelled for cheating and violence during three days of college entrance exams in May 1990. In 1995, in the first week of the national end-of-secondary-school exams, 4,000 candidates were expelled for cheating, and fifty teachers were fired for assisting candidates. The students' view that they have a right to cheat remains unchanged; and officials continue to deplore the ubiquity of exam misconduct in the country.[31]

Cheating in Cambodia has also been quite open and "normal." In Phnom Penh, Cambodia, in July 1996, hundreds of children scaled walls to pass notes to their friends taking high school entrance exams, despite the presence of more than 100 police officers who ringed the school in anticipation of the cheating. Even the army has been called in at times to try to control exam misconduct, but with little long-term effect:[32]

> Intimidation seems to have become more common and is now an unpleasant fact of life in several countries, including Nigeria, Pakistan, and Bangladesh. It can take many forms, including assaults of examination supervisory staff, destruction of a jeep by a mob unhappy with the presence of an examination board official in Baluchistan, placement of knives or guns on desks by candidates to deter close observation by supervisory staff, assault on an examination board chairman by a group (which included a politician) over his failure to change the location of an examination centre, and the storming of a centre by the wife of a government minister accompanied by a party of armed men to enable assistance to be given to her son. . . . In Nigeria . . . two invigilators . . . were taken out of the examination centre and shot dead by members of the community when they refused to co-operate in malpractice by candidates.[33]

Exam cheating may even be a form of political protest. One instance comes from Palestine. During the week ending 20 July 1990, high school seniors on the Israeli-occupied West Bank took final exams for admission to Jordanian and other universities. Blatant and widespread cheating was observed at many schools. Gangs of youths distributed photocopies of correct answers, gave answers over megaphones, and forced teachers to help students during the actual exam. This demonstration was arranged, it was believed, by Intifada activists, despite Hamas leaflets urging orderliness in exams.[34] In 1994, however, following the discovery that some exam papers had appeared in newspapers and that some exams were being sold for $10, strict security was imposed in Gaza. Police and Palestine National Guards were stationed at schools with instructions to examine candidates' identity cards and to arrest anyone attempting to disrupt the matriculation exams, which were due to be taken by an estimated 11,000 eighteen year olds. Penalties for cheating were announced: at least six months in jail.[35]

THEFTS AND LEAKS

Theft of questions and answers is another source of fraud. In the summer of 1989, padlocked boxes containing copies of New York State Regents exams were dispatched as usual from Albany to individual schools in New York City. After reports that test papers were being bought and sold in the city, the chemistry test was canceled. The *New York Post* published the story almost as it was going on, printing answers to questions and interviews with students who reported payments of anything from $10 to $2,000 for copies. A similar scandal involving the theft of exam papers had occurred in Los Angeles in 1988. In 1992, officials at Louisiana State University (LSU) uncovered an exam-for-sale business run by an employee of the university, Mr. Brent Wad Waldrop. Hundreds of LSU students had availed themselves of Mr. Waldrop's services, causing LSU to have to reissue the 1992 final spring exams.[36]

In South Africa, the provincial exams given at the end of secondary school (the "Matric" exams) have been plagued by reports of widespread buying and selling of question papers in the days and weeks leading up to the exam. In many cases the leaks of papers have been attributed to corrupt officials and clerks in the provincial departments of education, as well as to printers, transport intermediaries, and even principals and teachers. In 1996, the largest provincial department of education, Gauteng (which includes Johannesburg and Pretoria), transferred many of its employees in the exams division to other duties, targeting especially printing and packaging employees. The department feared not only that individual employees were leaking exam materials but that crime syndicates were at work. The question paper in accountancy was allegedly being sold for 2,000 rands (then worth about $600), causing the administration of the exam in that subject to be postponed to a later date to allow a fresh paper to be set. There were unsubstantiated reports that entire sets of exam papers for the Matric were available to purchase for 35,000 rands (about $10,000). In the following year, suspicion fell on "elite academics who drew up the exam papers. . . . [S]tatements from several accused pupils suggest examiners in at least two subjects could be implicated in the cheating. The province's examiners are drawn from its top state and independent schools, and universities," and the education minister blamed "the moral decay that exists where schools are driven by the glory of pass rates."[37]

While it was conceded that the problems of fraud in the Matric exams were not new, the department asserted that the new postapartheid administration was taking strong and effective action to end the corrupt practices. Education personnel who abet or condone cheating on the Matric exams, or who leak exam papers, are told that they will be punished with fines and prison terms. Students caught cheating will have to wait one year before being allowed to retake the exam.[38]

In China, university entrance exams are the prime means to distribute limited and valuable rewards to students as they ascend the educational and employment ladders. China, the birthplace of such public exams, has made major efforts to maintain fairness and security, but these have been undercut by cases of favoritism and downright criminality. In 1986, the State Education Commission announced new regulations and a campaign to crack down on fraud and nepotism. Serious offenders would face court prosecution, and staff would be dismissed for fraudulent practices. The whole process is more tense and competition is more cutthroat than in many other countries because opportunities for higher education are so much more limited and subject to political control.

At one time, educators who constructed the exams and graded the answers were sequestered for the months preceding and following administration of the tests, in order to maintain the highest degree of security. However, this practice was discontinued owing to its excessive cost in time and money.

Improprieties in China's state exam system, particularly favoritism and bribery, tend to discredit directly the educational system and reflect indirectly on the integrity of the political system. On a number of occasions, exam questions have been stolen or deliberately leaked for personal advantage or as exercises in distributing political favor to colleagues, friends, and family members. The national and provincial press uses such words as *selfish* and *dirty* to describe these acts and reports demands for severe punishment of individuals and party cadres involved in the process of "entering via the back door." Punishments imposed through party discipline include public confession of misdemeanors and crimes, dismissal from positions of authority, pay cuts, and expulsion from the Communist Party. Some individuals have been disqualified from the exams or expelled from the higher education institutions they had entered; others were arrested and received prison terms.[39] Even ETS had to cancel the scores of 30,000 Chinese candidates on the Graduate Record Examination (GRE) after it was revealed that a syndicate ring was selling the question papers.[40]

The persistence of exam fraud continues to be reported from China. In January 1998, Fudan University, Shanghai, had just expelled seven students found cheating in exams. In March 1998, sixty-six education officials and teachers in Guangxi Province were punished with jail terms and/or expulsion from the Communist Party, charged with accepting bribes to rig an exam. This was followed the next month by the Ministry of Education in Beijing convening a national video-phone conference, in which the ministry warned of its intention to crack down on rampant cheating in university entrance examinations.[41]

CONTROLS ON EXAM MISCONDUCT

Hiring an imposter to take the place of a weak candidate for an important exam is a relatively straightforward device. For example, in early October 1994, two first-year football players at the University of Southern California were under investigation for academic fraud, suspected of having someone take their college entrance exams for them. A similar case had been reported just one month before at the University of Houston.[42] College athletes have a higher risk than other students of being investigated for exam fraud. Universities will make an offer of an athletic scholarship conditional on the applicant gaining a specified minimum SAT score, and the rules of the National Collegiate Athletic Association require students to maintain a specified minimum grade point average. These requirements generate a considerable incentive for academically weak students to misbehave. In addition, because the athletic scholarship is usually well worth working for, students who have not done sufficiently well on the SAT are inclined to attend coaching courses and make extra academic efforts before they attempt the test a second time. Sometimes this effort pays off in terms of a sizeable increase in SAT scores, enough to trigger ETS review of their answer sheets.

While most incidents of impersonation bear all the hallmarks of an individual, one-off enterprise, exam fraud can be highly organized, even operating on conventional business lines. In November 1993, the *New York Times* reported the arrest of two Koreans who ran a company in the city called Total Test Center. The center provided impersonators to take tests in all kinds of public exams. The cost to have a substitute take the SAT was between $4,000 and $5,000; exams for a professional credential such as Certified Public Accountant reached the giddy heights of $40,000. The company supposedly even offered a contract for lifetime service to cover all the public exams one might possibly take in the future![43]

Passing a licensing test is required to operate as a stockbroker in New York State. In 1996, the National Association of Stockbrokers and Dealers announced that impersonation was rife in the licensing test. Substitutes were being paid as much as $2,500 to stand in for candidates. The association vowed to stamp out the practice, asserting that a photograph ID by itself would no longer be acceptable proof of identity. Henceforth, fingerprinting would be required as well.[44]

GRE scores are typically required by universities in the United States as part of the application for admission to many graduate study programs. Again in 1996 and in New York City, a GRE scam came to light—a sophisticated combination of electronic technology

and cheating. The scheme took advantage of the three-hour difference in clock time between the East and West Coasts of the United
States. Clients paid $6,000 a head—solid testimony to the impor-
tance of offering a good GRE score if an applicant hoped to be accepted in a "good" academic department at a "good" school. The
scheme worked as follows. Experts were assigned to take specific
parts of the test in New York, memorize the answers, and telephone them to West Coast collaborators. There, the answers were
coded into specially constructed electronic pencils, which were
given to the California candidates. Because of the three-hour time
difference, they had plenty of time to get to the exam hall, where
they could quietly consult their magic pencils for the recom-
mended response to each multiple-choice question.[45]

A variation on this basic theme occurred in 1997, when two Californian candidates, Mr. Danny Khatchaturian and Mr. Dikan Isk-
endarian, arranged to take the Law School Admissions Test (LSAT)
at a test center in Hawaii. Their scam depended on the two-hour
time difference between California and Hawaii. They paid an ac-
complice in California, Mr. Ashot Melikyan, $600 to snatch a copy
of the question booklet from an exam proctor at the start of the
LSAT session held at the University of Southern California. Threatening the proctor with a knife, Mr. Melikyan ran from the room
with the booklet. He handed it over to an expert on the law school
exam, who used an electronic pager to quickly transmit correct answers to Hawaii, where the two Californians were due to take the
test two hours later than Californian candidates. Unfortunately for
the enterprising would-be lawyers, their test results were just too
good—in fact, they were placed in the top 1 percent of the nearly
20,000 candidates taking the test that day. Their scam was detected,
and fines, prison terms, and probation periods followed.[46]

While $6,000, and even $600, is an impressive price to pay for
help on a university entrance exam, prices in the United States
have been low compared with those charged in Japan in recent
years. Except in the case of the most prestigious and selective institutions, college entrance is relatively easy to obtain in the United
States. The stakes are high but generally not the highest. This will
tend to hold down the price that fraudsters are willing to pay for
impersonators to take their exams for them. Japan, on the other
hand, has an education system that is driven by exams intended to
reward high academic achievement. Periodic national scandals in-

volving impersonation, theft, and fraud are the result of extreme pressure to enter the best institutions and obtain the rich future benefits flowing from a degree obtained at a top national (i.e., public) university such as Tokyo University or an outstanding private institution. Teruhisa Horio, a noted Japanese scholar and writer on education, has cited scandals that have arisen in Japan not only over the sale of exam questions but also over bribes offered and taken to gain entrance to medical schools, despite the applicants having poor marks on the entrance exams.[47]

In the early 1990s, for example, corrupt university officials were discovered to have guaranteed students admission to their institution. They hired bright undergraduates to take the Meiji University entrance exams in the place of wealthy applicants "with dubious qualifications," and some of the officials were arrested. Many of the imposters were students from Waseda University, possibly the most prestigeful of the private universities in Japan. Police say parents paid $100,000 or more to hire substitutes for their children, a vast price differential over anything reported from the United States. Moreover, the use of "brokers" who are in the business of supplying impersonators is thought to be widespread. At least twenty cases were recently discovered, suggesting that this practice has been going on for years and is not limited to Meiji University. Two officials were arrested for taking $50,000 to pass a rich businessman's son, who was subsequently expelled. In yet another case, police arrested the principal and a teacher at the oldest high school in Hyogo Prefecture for altering the entrance exam answers of fifteen students.[48]

Corruption of the university entrance process can be a matter of straightforward bribery—at least, that is how it appeared to many an anxious parent in the Soviet Union. A medical school professor tells the following story in his autobiography:

> Dr. Egalevich's only son was eighteen. The next year he applied for admission to our medical school. His father had been beside himself with anxiety the whole previous year, tormented by the question: will he be admitted or not? Any time he met me, he interrogated me with questions like these:
> "What's the Jewish quota at your school?"
> "I should grease a palm or two? I mean now; later I'll give more."
> "They say your Belousov [the dean] accepts bribes from entrants. I'd be glad to pay him, only how should I approach him?"[49]

RULES, REGULATIONS, AND CONSEQUENCES OF CHEATING

"Silence! No talking, please." The proctor's voice cuts through the air:

> You have ninety minutes for this exam. When I announce that time is up, please put down your pens and pencils and close your booklets. Let me remind you that cheating is a serious offence and may result in offenders being expelled from the exam room and having their papers canceled. Do not attempt to speak to one another, or look over others' work, or refer to illicit material brought into the room. Remember that criminal charges may be brought against candidates who cheat or commit fraud. Now, please open your question paper and begin.

Anyone who has taken an important external exam will recall some of the conventions. Candidates may have to prove their identity before entering the exam room; their papers are identified by number rather than name. They will be seated far enough apart so that they cannot read a neighbor's work. To start the exam, an invigilator will remove the question papers from a sealed envelope and, at the end, duly pack and seal the answers for dispatch to the examiners.

Such common experiences are not merely due to convention or happenstance. They are some of the measures intended to ensure fairness and to control cheating. Exam authorities usually publish rules and regulations intended to maintain security before, during, and after the exam. They often state required procedures, define possible offences, and specify the consequences of what are euphemistically described as "unfair practices."

Some actions may even be regarded as criminal. For example, the University of London School Examinations Board "reserves the right to refuse the admission of a candidate to examinations within the purview of the Board if it is satisfied that the candidate has been involved in any serious irregularity, misconduct or dishonesty in connection with the examinations conducted by another examining body."[50] Moreover, the board requires school principals when submitting names of candidates to inform them of those who are closely related to themselves or to members of the teaching, secretarial, and other staff of the school.

All irregularities must be reported to the board, and the superintendent of the exam is empowered to discontinue the exam of candidates who engage in misconduct. They should only be expelled from the room "when it is felt that such disciplinary action is essential." Unauthorized material brought in by candidates must be deposited with the superintendent and may be handed over to the board ("Candidates may not take blotting paper or paper of any description into the exam room"). Communication among candidates and copying are forbidden. The board may withhold publication of the results for candidates suspected of irregularities or misconduct pending investigation. Candidates may be disqualified and barred from further board exams if the board finds that they have been involved in any irregularity, misconduct, or dishonesty. Candidates are advised that impersonation or attempted impersonation may lead to criminal proceedings. Material copied directly from books without attribution, as part of coursework or projects submitted for exams, "will be regarded as an act of deliberate deception which may result in disqualification or disqualification and disbarment." The senate may revoke any credential if at any time it is discovered (and proven) that there was any irregularity in the events or circumstances leading to the granting of that credential. Further, anyone involved in irregularity, dishonesty, or fraud may be barred from future entry.

In France, a popular paperback covering information about the *baccalauréat* exam and various kinds of advice to candidates reminds them that from the very earliest days of the exam at the beginning of the nineteenth century, students were reported to have written their Latin or Greek declensions on their shirt cuffs. Nowadays, advances in technology may include the use of radio or other devices. But, test takers are warned, "if tempted to cheat, be aware that there are big risks: first, you will immediately be excluded from the exam; then you will be judged by a disciplinary group that can forbid you from any public exam for a period of as much as five years."[51]

The regulations governing conduct in the French *baccalauréat* are issued by the Ministry of Education and are, as one might expect, clear, unambiguous, and strict. Each candidate must produce an identity card with a photo (student card, passport, or driver's license). Before taking the exam, they must complete and sign a declaration that they have been warned of the legal consequences of false signatures, other frauds, and attempts at fraud. Once admitted to the exam hall, they may not communicate with one another or with others outside the room or have with them any papers, notes, or books except what is authorized. The candidate will be excluded from the exam hall if he or she commits a flagrant offence; a duly appointed jury of educators is empowered to adjudicate and will determine if a candidate's exam is to be invalidated.

Colleges, universities, and many secondary schools have formal statements about the conduct expected of students in their coursework and exams. The University of Calgary, Canada, publishes a detailed "statement on student plagiarism, etc.":

2. Cheating is an extremely serious academic offence. Cheating at tests or exams includes but is not limited to dishonest or attempted dishonest conduct such as speaking to other candidates or communicating with them under any circumstances whatsoever; bringing into the examination room any textbook, notebook, memorandum, other written material or mechanical or electronic device not authorized by the examiner; writing an examination or part of it, or consulting any person or materials outside the confines of the examination room without permission to do so, or leaving answer papers exposed to view, or persistent attempts to read other students' examination papers.

3. Other Academic Misconduct—other academic misconduct includes, but is not limited to, tampering or attempts to tamper with examination scripts, class work, grades and/or class records; failure to abide by directions by an instructor regarding the individuality of work handed in; the acquisition, attempted acquisition, possession, and/or distribution of examination materials or information not authorized by the instructor; the impersonation of another student in an examination or other class assignment; the falsification or fabrication of clinical or laboratory reports; the non-authorized tape recording of lectures. All of these offences are extremely serious.

4. Any student who voluntarily and consciously aids another student in the commission of one of these offences is also guilty of academic misconduct.

Penalties for misconduct range from award of a failing grade, through suspension from the university, to expulsion. Provision is even made for laying criminal charges against an offender:

Academic Misconduct—Criminal Offence[.] Where there is a criminal act involved in plagiarism, cheating or other academic misconduct, e.g., theft (taking another student's paper from his/her possession, or from the possession of a faculty member without permission), breaking and entering (forcibly entering an office to gain access to paper, grades or records), forgery, personation and conspiracy (impersonating another student by agreement and writing his/her paper) and other such offences under the Criminal Code of Canada, the University may take legal advice on the appropriate response and, where appropriate, refer the matter to the police, in addition to or in substitution for any action taken under these regulations by the university.[52]

In the United States, state laws concerning credentials and public exams may similarly define infractions and specify penalties for offences, including cheating in public exams and falsification of exam-based records and credentials. In Massachusetts, for example, the penalty for selling an exam paper or sitting an exam in another's place is a fine of $100 or six months of imprisonment. In New York, offences such as disclosure of exam questions set by the State Board of Regents are subject to a fine (but only a mere $50) or thirty days of imprisonment. Sitting an exam in another's place may be punished by a fine of up to $1,000 and/or up to one year of imprisonment. For the most part, courts in the United States and elsewhere are reluctant to impose any severe punishment on individual exam cheaters or impersonators—as distinct from organized, commercial schemes, for which they will usually take a much tougher line.

Courts will sometimes overturn the sanctions that school and exam authorities have imposed on cheaters. An unusual case occurred in Italy in 1996. Council of State judges heard a case in which a secondary school student took out some math notes during the *maturita* exam and was immediately caught before having a chance to use the information or hand in his paper. The exam authorities declared the student's exam paper to be invalid, by reason of cheating. The student went to court, and the judges held that no sufficient offence had been committed to warrant cancellation of the student's exam and that the exam paper was therefore valid. The president of the Italian headmasters' association was predictably not amused by what he reportedly held to be unwarranted judicial interference in purely scholastic affairs.[53]

A long-running complaint by a British student about his university's procedures in a case of cheating began in 1986 and had not ended even by 1999. Francis Foecke was an older student in computer science and mathematics at Bristol University from 1983 to 1986. His thirteen final exam papers appeared to his examiners to be so brilliant that they were too good to be true. The university accused him of "dishonest conduct" and awarded him only an ordinary degree instead of the honors degree to which his exam results would normally have entitled him. Foecke exhausted all his avenues of appeal against that decision—within the university, to the university's "Visitor" (Queen Elizabeth herself!), and in the British courts of justice. The High Court required him to deposit £25,000 (about $40,000) as security against future legal costs that might be awarded against him. Foecke did not have the money, so the court threw out his case: "Foecke claims the university violated his right under Article 4 of the European Convention on Human Rights to a hearing before an independent and impartial tribunal. . . . A university spokesman said: 'The university continues to hold its view . . . that he breached the university's exam procedures.'" Now the case is going to the European Court of Human Rights, in Strasbourg, France.[54]

The top administrators of universities and exam organizations are probably not too happy with judicial oversight of their operations, but far worse problems can face educators who take a stand against cheating. In 1995, it is reported, a teacher in Bangladesh was hacked to death after trying to stop cheating in the end-of-secondary-school exams![55]

In the United States, private agencies such as the ETS serve as the major purveyors of external exams. ETS makes its own security arrangements along similar lines to those of other examining authorities in the United States and abroad. The organization takes great pains to maintain high levels of security of its questions, which is hardly surprising considering that its databanks of questions have been field tested and subjected to extensive reliability and validity testing at considerable expense. They represent very valuable intellectual property. The organization's heavy reliance on multiple-choice tests and electronic grading of answer sheets accounts for its emphasis on the security of its stock of questions and specific test papers. ETS routinely compares answer papers in order to uncover suspected cases of cheating and may require candidates to retake the test. However, determined cheaters do not find it too difficult to circumvent ETS controls.

Mr. Larry Adler was caught because of a tip-off, rather than by any routine ETS procedures, such as comparing the candidate's face with the picture on the driver's license or analyzing the candidate's pattern of answers. In 1991, Mr. Adler, who had a poor high school record, obtained excellent SAT scores. He had employed a substitute to take the exam for him. Unfortunately for him, he could not keep his mouth shut and boasted to classmates about his scheme. One of them tipped off ETS, which arranged for an analysis of handwriting specimens. The three members of the ETS review board concluded that Mr. Adler had not taken the test himself. He was offered a choice: retake the test, submit to arbitration, provide additional information, cancel the score, or have ETS send the questioned score to colleges with an explanation of why it had been questioned. Mr. Adler rejected all of the options offered and later sued ETS for not releasing the scores. Although Mr. Adler testified that he had taken the test, Mr. David Farmer, a first-year student at the University of Virginia, later admitted that he had been paid $200 to take the exam in Mr. Adler's place. Mr. Adler was subsequently convicted of perjury and served a brief jail term.[56]

In a similar case, Mr. Brian Dalton, also an SAT candidate, sued ETS for release of his scores. Mr. Dalton took the test twice in 1991, once in May and then again in November. His combined score increased by 410 points. Because the increase was greater than 350 points, ETS automatically reviewed his answer papers, concluding that the handwriting on the two sets was different. Their document expert gave the opinion that the May and November papers were completed by different persons. ETS then informed Mr. Dalton that it had made a preliminary decision to cancel his November score because of the handwriting difference. At the same time, ETS informed him of five options: supply additional information, retake the test, have the scores canceled with refund of fees, permit third-party review by any institution receiving the scores, or submit to arbitration. All of these options were cited in the Registration Bulletin for the SAT, and when he registered for the November exam, Mr. Dalton had agreed to the conditions set out in the bulletin.

Mr. Dalton elected the first option and submitted further information in the form of a number of documents: verification that he was suffering from mononucleosis during the May examination; diagnostic test results from a preparatory course he took prior to the November examination (he had taken no similar course prior

to the May SAT) that were consistent with his performance on that
test; a statement by an ETS proctor who remembered Dalton's presence during the November examination; and statements from two
students, one of whom was previously unacquainted with Dalton,
that he had been in the classroom during that test. Mr. Dalton further provided ETS with a report from a document examiner re-
tained by his family who concluded that he was the author of both
sets of answer sheets.

Despite all this, ETS held fast to its previous decision, stating that
it would continue to question the November scores and would continue to withhold them. Brian's father sued for release of the scores
and won judgments against ETS in the trial court and in the appel-
late division. In their decisions, both courts criticized the testing
agency for breaching its contract with Mr. Dalton by not acting in
good faith and specifically by refusing to consider various pieces of
evidence produced by Mr. Dalton to counter the ETS contention
that he had cheated. ETS appealed to New York State's highest
court, the Court of Appeals. In December 1995, in a 6–2 decision
that court accepted that ETS had breached its contract with Brian
Dalton (by not considering the additional documentation produced) but overturned the lower courts' orders to ETS to release
the scores. The majority of the judges held that the ETS obligation
to Mr. Dalton was to consider carefully all the additional information provided, given that it was germane to the question of
whether or not Mr. Dalton had taken the test himself. ETS had not
done that. On the other hand, "Dalton is not . . . entitled to release
of his score as though fully validated. . . . [T]he validity of Dalton's
November SAT score has yet to be determined. . . . Dalton is entitled to relief that comports with ETS' contractual promise—good
faith consideration of the material he submitted to ETS." Accordingly, ETS was ordered to consider the additional information supplied, which it did.[57] But (according to Mr. Dalton's lawyers) ETS
stood by its earlier determination that Mr. Dalton had not taken the
SAT himself the second time, and the testing organization therefore
refused to release his scores.

Over the years, ETS has been accused of consistently violating
professional standards in the way it handles cases of suspected student misconduct. It became the target of a variety of charges of civil
offences such as ignoring "due process" and systematic abuse of
civil rights, to say nothing of bias and prejudice.[58]

In its constant search for more secure procedures, in November 1993, ETS introduced new computerized tests for entry to graduate studies (the GRE). These were claimed to be virtually impregnable with regard to cheating. However, Kaplan Educational Centers, a large private coaching company, suspected that it was easy to cheat, notwithstanding ETS claims of effective security. They had three employees go undercover to take the tests, memorize questions, and construct a replica of the exam. This was then taken to ETS, which found 70–80 percent correspondence with the original test. As a result ETS suspended the next round of computer-based tests. The potential for cheating appeared to have increased with the new tests because they may be used frequently, there are fewer versions, and thus the same questions appear more often. Noteworthy, too, is the fact that Kaplan apparently had no great difficulty in circumventing controls on imposture.

APPROACHES TO CHEATING

Exam cheating exists, so much we know. It is universal, but it is difficult to estimate its precise extent. Rules, security measures, and threats of serious consequences are apparently not enough to stem its growth, let alone eliminate it altogether. For some individuals, the expected gain, that is, the prize for good results, is so tempting and so valuable that it outweighs expected costs—financial in some instances, penal in others, moral in all cases.

The difficulties in dealing with the problems of exam cheating are in some places simply a result of the vastness of the enterprise. The University of Bombay handbook for 1984 on the proper conduct of public exams notes that it conducts over 400 exams per year, covering one-quarter of a million students, in about 120 exam centers. Despite numerous publications, workshops, and seminars on how to organize exams, and legislation intended to control cheating, there has been no noticeable improvement in India.[59]

If cheating cannot be eliminated entirely from academic life, can its incidence be reduced? What can and should faculty and college administrators do in addition to what they are already doing? How much deterrence is worth how much control and change in current academic arrangements?

There are two schools of thought on the matter. One approach favors an emphasis on sanctions. Colleges and instructors should be explicit about the standards of integrity and honesty they expect students to meet with respect to their coursework, tests, and exams. There should be frequent warnings, accompanied by information on the specific penalties that will be applied to cheaters. Laws that make it too easy for those accused of cheating to drag institutions and instructors through the courts should be repealed or weakened, otherwise the fear of litigation will probably undermine any resolute campaign against cheating. Some institutions have adopted honor codes, by which students must affirm their intention to eschew cheating and, under some codes, even act as whistleblowers when they observe cheating by fellow students.

Another approach recommends minimizing opportunities to cheat, organizing coursework and exams so that it is just much more difficult to cheat. Minimizing the opportunities to cheat, it is held, is more ethical than being lax in the organization of coursework so that students are tempted to cheat. Access to Internet resources is making it more necessary and urgent to have students present their work for course papers in stages: proposal, outline, first draft, redraft as necessary, final submission. In this way, it will be more difficult to use the services of a term paper "mill" or Internet sources. In addition, tests should reduce items relying on the recall of facts and emphasize instead questions and problems that require understanding, analysis, and application. Providing more frequent, smaller tests, rather than fewer, larger tests, as well as providing opportunities to retake tests that have turned out poorly, it is argued, will reduce the incentives and opportunities to cheat. If multiple-choice items are used, the order of questions should be scrambled; and not all test papers need to have the same selection of questions. One instructor uses open-book exams, with an emphasis on applications-type questions, and writes the following message on the chalkboard during tests:

TOP FIVE REASONS NOT TO COPY FROM YOUR NEIGHBOR
1. It is immoral and unethical!
2. You'll deprive yourself of the satisfaction of your own accomplishment!
3. You can copy from your own book and notes instead!
4. Your neighbor probably knows less than you do!
5. Your neighbor is taking a different test anyway![60]

A study done in the early 1990s provides some empirical, as distinct from hortatory, advice on the subject. The researchers surveyed 600 students at two public universities in twelve economics classes, each with a different instructor. Students were guaranteed anonymity and were asked if they had cheated in class. Characteristics of each class that might have affected the students' behavior were then recorded: number and type of tests given, academic rank of the instructors, amount of class space per student, students' grade point averages, and so forth. The most important class characteristic associated with cheating was instructor's rank—students whose instructors were graduate assistants were 30+ percent more likely to cheat than students with instructors who were full professors. Three practices that were correlated with substantial reductions in cheating were providing multiple versions of tests (25 percent reduction), giving a verbal warning against cheating at the time of the test (13 percent reduction), and using an additional proctor (11 percent reduction). Two things that did not appear to affect cheating much if at all were avoiding multiple-choice questions and widely separating students.[61]

It seems that most faculty members do not take positive steps to deter cheating. They would rather assume that their students are basically honest. Malcolm Milne, a retired British Colonial Office administrator, tells the following story in his memoirs:

> We wrote the Ibo papers in premises belonging to the Church Missionary Society under the supervision of a good missionary canon. So transparent was his own honesty and so obviously did he believe in ours that he left us entirely unsupervised for long periods. In the Unseen Translation paper one of our number said, ". . . this is a damn long paper. Blunt, you do the first paragraph, Robin the second and third and Milne the fourth . . ." dividing it up amongst us.
>
> Some weeks later, after we'd all heard that we'd passed, Angus Robin and I met the good canon at a function in Onitsha. Commenting on our performance in the exam he said, "You all did very well, really; except possibly for the unseen translation. There you all . . . I can't think why . . . made the same very odd mistake in the fourth paragraph."[62]

Many institutions of higher education publish formal statements urging their instructors to take seriously the possibility of cheating by students and not to look the other way when cheating is suspected. One of the most comprehensive of such statements, with an excellent listing of steps that can be taken to prevent cheating on tests, exams, and other academic assignments, is by Barbara Davies at the University of California at Berkeley, entitled "Preventing Academic Dishonesty," and can be found at www.uga.berkeley. edu/sled/bgd/prevent.html. Instructors who heed such messages can employ some fairly sophisticated statistical tools to help them. In the United States, where multiple-choice, machine-scorable tests are common, there has been growing use of computer programs to detect cheating. The programs compare patterns of answers across students; the more sophisticated programs are even capable of associating the results with class seating charts. The instructor is alerted to particular patterns that have a very low probability of occurring by chance. It is then up to the instructor to decide what to do about students whose answer sheets have been singled out.[63] Certainly, any tendency to jump to invidious conclusions should be held in check: "No mechanistic detection method currently available can provide reliable evidence of cheating. Statistical evidence alone should not be used to accuse individuals of cheating, . . . since it cannot conclusively prove that cheating took place."[64]

CAN WE TRUST EXAMS?

In September 1999, ETS joined with the Advertising Council to begin a major three-year advertising campaign to discourage academic cheating. Broadcast and print ads are targeted at middle school students (ages eleven to thirteen years) across the nation, as this is reckoned to be the age when academic cheating behavior becomes evident. ETS hopes that "sending a clear message to these children about the negative consequences of cheating will help to discourage this serious societal behavior."[65] Whether we are seeing more cheating on exams because moral standards have slipped among the young population is a debatable point, and whether the ETS campaign will have any discernible effect remains to be seen. What we do know is that cheating threatens public confidence in the efficiency and legitimacy of external exam systems. It is a form of sabotage: It undercuts the candidate, the teacher, and, in fact, the whole system of selection, evaluation, and rewards. Yet exams persist, marked by intense competition for good results. Other means are available and are often used as alternatives or supplements to exams in order to assess candidates for graduation and entry to courses of study and subsequent careers: interviews, recommendations, examples of schoolwork, or profiles of school experience. These, too, have their inherent deficiencies and are open to dishonest practices: Judgments are naturally subjective, prone to bias and prejudice, open to manipulation and unfair personal advantage.

We rely on exams to provide "objective" measures of ability—usually to counteract favoritism (or discrimination) based on birth, wealth, social position, physical appearance, race, religion, deportment, and so forth. So far, no better substitute has been widely adopted to assess learning and performance and to distribute the valuable prizes so often associated with exam success. Despite a keener sense of how their purposes may be subverted, exams are more in vogue than ever. Once, only a small number of people took them and for limited purposes. Nowadays, as access to higher reaches of education increases, as larger numbers participate, and as certification and licensing control access to more and more occupations, exams of one kind or another are increasingly common. Consequently, concern about their reliability and fairness has come more to the fore than when they affected only the few. The crucial question for parents, teachers, candidates, employers, government officials, and citizens is, How far can an exam system be trusted? An acceptable degree of trust is only possible if all these players see the system as basically fair. And that requires public confidence that only the smallest probability exists of irregularities, misconduct, fraud, and criminality that might tarnish the exam and credentialing process.

NOTES

1. C. M. Bowra, *Memories 1898–1939* (London: Weidenfeld and Nicolson, 1966), 150–51.

2. See http://shaungpro.tripod.com/tips.html, Internet.

3. Michael Moffat, "Undergraduate Cheating," ERIC document ED334921, 1990.

4. Aleza Spalter and Leonard Saxe, "Everybody (Else) Does It: Academic Cheating," ERIC document ED347931, 1992.

5. Sheilah Maramark and Mindi Barth Maline, *Academic Dishonesty among College Students* (Washington, D.C.: Office of Educational Research and Improvement, 1993).

6. Donald L. McCabe and Linda Klebe Trevino, "What We Know about Cheating in College: Longitudinal Trends and Recent Developments," *Change* 28(1) 1996: 28–33.

7. George M. Diekhoff, E. E. LaBeff, R. E. Clark, L. E. Williams, B. Francis, and V. I. Haines, "College Cheating Ten Years Later," *Research in Higher Education* 37(4) 1996: 487–502.

8. See "Cheating and Succeeding: Record Numbers of Top High School Students Take Ethical Shortcut," 29th Annual Survey of High Achievers, 1998, conducted under the auspices of *Who's Who among American High School Students*.

9. David Owen, *None of the Above: Behind the Myth of Scholastic Aptitude* (Boston: Houghton Mifflin, 1985), 141.

10. Stewart Ugelow, "Standardized Mess: Students Know It's Easy to Cheat on SAT," *Washington Post*, 3 January 1993.

11. Douglas Frantz and Jon Nordheimer, "Giant of Exam Business Keeps Quiet on Cheating," *New York Times*, 28 September 1997: 1, 32.

12. Michael Moore, *Cheating 101: The Benefits and Fundamentals of Earning the Easy A* (Berkeley Heights, N.J.: Moore Publishing Company, 1991).

13. "For No-Cheating Vows, Discount at Stores," *New York Times*, 5 March 1997.

14. Roger Bushby, "Internet Essays Cause Degrees of Concern," *Times Educational Supplement*, 17 October 1997, Internet.

15. *Times Educational Supplement*, 21 March 1995: 16.

16. *Times Educational Supplement*, 28 July 1955: 11; GCE A-level candidate, letter, 1995.

17. Jennifer Lee, "Powerful Calculators Throw Teachers a New Curve," *New York Times*, 2 September 1999: G1, G7.

18. John Croucher, *Exam Scams* (London: Allen and Unwin, 1997).

19. Jamie Wilson, "Students Used Email to Cheat," *Guardian*, 14 August 1999, Internet.

20. "Cheating Rife in the Universities," *Independent on Sunday*, 12 September 1999, Internet.

21. Chris Mihill, "Cheating Rife among University Students," *Guardian*, 26 March 1994: 1, 6.

22. This study was done at Edith Cowan University, Perth. Reported in Geoff Maslin, "Cheats with Pagers and Cordless Radio Cribs," *Times Educational Supplement*, 11 October 1966, Internet.

23. Vladimir Golyakhovsky, *Russian Doctor* (London: Robert Hale, 1984), 258–59.

24. Yulia Poltorak, "Cheating Behavior among Students of Four Moscow Universities," *Higher Education* 30(2) September 1995: 225–46.

25. "Copy, Comrades," *New York Times*, 25 December 1995–1 January 1996: 26–27.

26. H. R. F. Keating, *Cheating Death* (New York: Mysterious Books, 1992), 16.

27. Barbara Crossette, "Vast Cheating Forces Many in India to Retake Scholastic Test," *New York Times*, 2 January 1990: A10:2.

28. "Kashmir Cheating Clampdown," *Times Higher Education Supplement*, 31 January 1992: 9.

29. John Zubrzycki, "Exam Cheating Law Fails to Calm Furious Opposition," *South China Morning Post*, 31 March 1998: 14.

30. Chuck Shepherd, "Update," *Optimist* (University of Massachusetts at Amherst), 12–18 September 1996: 34.

31. Croucher, *Exam Scams*.

32. Shepherd, "Update"; Seth Mydans, "Armed and Ready for War on Cheating Students," *New York Times*, 26 July 1997.

33. Vincent Greany and Thomas Kellaghan, "The Integrity of Public Examinations in Developing Countries," in H. Goldstein and T. Lewis, eds., *Assessment: Problems, Developments and Statistical Issues* (New York: John Wiley and Sons, 1996), 173–74.

34. Joel Brinkley, "'Anarchy' of Cheating Hits Palestinian Schools," *New York Times*, 22 July 1990: 1, 4.

35. "Cheat at Exams and Risk Going to Prison," *Times Educational Supplement*, 17 June 1994: 18.

36. "LSU Discloses Cheating Plot: University Worker Arrested," *Times-Picayune*, 15 May 1992: B4.

37. Andy Duffy, "Exam Cheats Finger Examiners," *Weekly Mail and Guardian*, 10 January 1997, Internet.

38. Joshua Amupadhi, Stuart Hess, and David Shapshak, "Matric Exam Leaks 'Plugged,'" *Weekly Mail and Guardian*, 1 November 1996, Internet; Karen MacGregor, "Cheat-Proof Exams in the Pipeline," *Times Educational Supplement*, 21 February 1997, Internet.

39. "Chinese Crackdown on Exam Fraudsters," *Times Higher Education Supplement*, 25 July 1986: 8. See also "Bu Zheng Zhi Feng" ("Corruption in Education"), *Chinese Education* 24 (winter 1991–92)—the entire issue is devoted to this topic.

40. Douglas Frantz and Jon Nordheimer, "Giant of Exam Business Keeps Quiet on Cheating," *New York Times*, 28 September 1997: 1, 32.

41. "Leash Cheating on Exams," *China Daily*, 15 April 1998, Internet.

42. Elliot Almond and Greg Sandoval, "Two USC Players Challenged on Entrance Exam Results," *Los Angeles Times*, 1 October 1994: C1, C3; "How Could This Be?" *Houston Chronicle*, 8 September 1994: B4.

43. Michael Winerip, "Two Arrested in Scheme to Pass Tests," *New York Times*, 23 November 1993: B3.

44. Floyd Norris, "Licensing-Test Cheaters Face N.A.S.D. Ban: Dozens of Stockbrokers Said to Have Paid Examination Stand-Ins," *New York Times*, 10 July 1996: D2.

45. "Under Cover Agents Cap Exam Cheating Scheme," *China Morning Post*, 30 October 1996.

46. "2 Men to Serve Year at Home for Law School Exam Caper," *Los Angeles Times*, 25 March 2000, Internet.

47. Teruhisa Horio, *Educational Thought and Ideology in Modern Japan: State Authority and Intellectual Freedom* (Tokyo: University of Tokyo Press, 1988), 302.

48. "Charges Lead to More Fears of Corruption," *Times Educational Supplement*, 19 July 1991: 9; "Japan Exam Probe Reveals Proxy Fraud," *Times Educational Supplement*, 16 August 1991: 11.

49. Golyakhovsky, *Russian Doctor*, 210–11.

50. University of London School Examinations Board, *General Certificate of Education: Regulations and Syllabuses, June 1989–January 1990* (London: University of London, 1987), Regulation 3.6.

51. Jean-Pierre Jacques, *Bacs: Mode d'emploi* (Paris: Hatier, 1994), 106.

52. University of Calgary Statement on Student Plagiarism, etc., http://www.ucalgary.ca/UofC/departments/SECRETARIAT3/app-acc.htm, Internet.

53. "Cheating Pupil Acquitted," *Times Educational Supplement*, 27 September 1996, Internet.

54. Peter Kingston, "Honesty on Trial," *Guardian*, 31 August 1999, Internet.

55. Croucher, *Exam Scams.*

56. Stewart Ugelow, "Standardized Mess: Students Know It's Easy to Cheat on SAT," *Washington Post*, 3 January 1993: B3.

57. *Peter Dalton, &C., Respondent, v. Educational Testing Service, &C., Appellant*, 87 N.Y.2d 384, 663 N.E.2d 289, 639 N.Y.S.2d 977, 7 December 1995.

58. Owen, *None of the Above.*

59. Mathew Zachariah, "Examination Reform in Traditional Universities: A Few Steps Forward, Many Steps Back," *Higher Education* 26 (1993): 115–46.

60. "Should Faculty Take a Bolder Stand against Student Cheating?" *On Campus*, May–June 1988: 4; Leslie Ault, "Top Five Reasons Not to Cheat," *On Campus*, September 1988: 15.

61. Joe Kerkvliet, "Cheating by Economics Students: A Comparison of Survey Results," *Journal of Economic Education* 25 (Spring 1994): 121–33.

62. Malcolm Milne, *No Telephone to Heaven: From Apex to Nadir—Colonial Service in Nigeria, Aden, the Cameroons and the Gold Coast, 1938–61* (Longstock, Hants, U.K.: Meon Hill Press, 1999), 80.

63. David Harp, "Big Prof Is Watching You," *Discover* 12 (April 1991): 12–13.

64. David J. Dwyer and Jeffrey B. Hecht, "Cheating Detection: Statistical, Legal, and Policy Implications," ERIC Document No. ED382066, 1994.

65. ETS, letter, 16 July 1999.

Chapter 3

Credentials Fraud

Credential: (Usually in pl.) Letters or written warrants commending or entitling the bearer to credit or confidence.

The world of postsecondary education, once limited in size and scope, is now enormous. UNESCO has estimated that as of 1996 enrollment in postsecondary education worldwide totaled about 1.13 billion.[1] No single person can claim thorough knowledge of all of the institutions, programs, and personnel, even in his or her own area of specialization. In contemporary societies, personal recommendations, once heavily relied on, are now regarded as unreliable and suspect, prone to bias. Formal credentials are universally demanded.

As formal education reaches more and more people in more countries of the world, the complexity of career paths increases. Schools and employers prefer to rely on impersonal and bureaucratic records such as certificates and diplomas from recognized institutions rather than on personal and more informal recommendations. Such documents are relied on to be authoritative and objective evidence that the holder has passed specified exams, acquired certain skills or experience, and gained access to advanced training or professional status.

Credentials, therefore, have value and serve in the economist's jargon as positional or status goods: They are goods priced according to their power to position their owners in society or to express some view of who or what they are. For this reason, if for no other, the demand for formal credentials is great and growing. But, alongside the growing use of legitimate credentials to move toward

61

higher levels of education and training, to obtain employment, and to achieve social status, illicit ways of obtaining genuine credentials, as well as legal ways of obtaining fraudulent credentials, have proliferated.

Credentials fraud is by no means a new phenomenon. The Library of Congress has a collection of photocopies of false diplomas bought by a representative of the *Philadelphia Record* newspaper in 1880 for $455 (a sum worth perhaps $20,000 in today's money).[2] Fraud remains alive and well, is hard to suppress, and continues to grow in seriousness and frequency. The reasons are not hard to discern. In the United States, anyone who applies for a job, skilled or unskilled, as engineer or supermarket checkout clerk, as lawyer or salesperson, finds that an educational credential, even if only a high school diploma, is expected.

But legitimate postsecondary credentials are expensive. Tuition fees and books for undergraduate study cost anywhere between $2,000 and $20,000 a year. Many colleges now require students to bring computers. Living expenses away from home can add $6,000 to $12,000. Graduate study for professional qualifications means another one to four years of similar, or greater, expense. By the time a graduate walks onto the stage at commencement exercises to receive the diploma for, say, an MBA, a law degree, or a master's in electrical engineering, the required six to seven years of postsecondary education could easily have absorbed $100,000 and maybe even $200,000 of direct, out-of-pocket costs. And that figure does not include the potential income from employment forgone while studying! It is a tribute to the perceived (and largely realized) advantages associated with possession of such expensive credentials that the demand for them not only is high but increases year by year.

Nor is the demand by any means confined to the United States. In many countries, opportunities for postsecondary education are severely limited not only by high costs relative to personal incomes but also by a historic lack of availability of postsecondary education. Yet educational credentials are fully as important abroad as they are in the United States—perhaps even more so. In addition, U.S. credentials, especially from graduate professional education, enjoy high prestige abroad—witness the over half-million overseas students currently studying in the United States.

This strong demand for educational credentials at home and abroad, together with the very high costs of obtaining them, produces ideal conditions for fraudulent practice. Why undertake the expense and effort needed to obtain honest credentials when good-looking (even if bogus) certificates are readily available at much less cost in dollars, effort, and personal inconvenience? This was the motivation expressed by one inquirer who posted an Internet notice on the Flight Instructors Message Board in February 1999. The following discussion includes the full exchange of information and views verbatim: "If there's anyone out there that has got any information about this college [Pacific Western University] I would appreciate the feedback. This is a non accrediated college but they say the airlines don't care, and it will work like any ordinary degree. To work for the Airlines does your degree have to be accrediated? Thanks for the info. Robert." Robert did not have long to wait for advice. G. Davis told him,

I have met pilots who have gotten on with the Majors with non-accredited degrees with colleges like Western Pacific. When I asked major airline reps at an Air Inc Job Fair, some said accredited and some said any degree is better then none.

Since I already had an AA degree, it was a hard choice between finishing a four year degree in four months with a non-accredited or do an accredited program th[r]ough distant learning. I am going the latter. It cost more and takes more time, but as I take these courses, I figure if I am going to get the degree it will be for me. I don't see how fo[u]r months for a BS degree at Western Pacific, is equivalent to the full course load I am enduring through this distant learning college.

By the way, I started with Embry-Riddle for the first year, but it got too expensive. If you look up distant learning on the web you will see that a lot of Universities and Colleges, offer these programs now.

My point is, call the airlines you are applying to and ask them. Then ask yourself. Do I want this degree from an accredited college or not. Or can I just go to Kinko's and have them make up a fancy for $1.20. Good luck

But different advice was provided, too: "Whowever told you that was lying. Having an accrediated college degree is the only way to make it to the majors, however saying that if you only want to fly for a regional they could care less about the degree." And even something quite encouraging was offered: "I have a friend that received his degree from them and went on to fly for UsAir and is now flying for FedEx as a FO on a 727. All they care about is a degree. He was asked in his interview why he finished his degree through them and he explained that in order to flight instruct and keep his career moving that he needed the flexiblilty of this type of school. hope this helps you out." But the final message in this exchange delivered the coup de grâce: "Paciffic Western Univeristy was rated as the worst non tradition university to get a degree from. Try Other school's Like Columbia State University or Columbia Southern University. For more info on these schools check out the Popular Mechanics Magazine, under classifieds (education)."

DIPLOMA MILLS

In 1984, the FBI estimated that there were at least 100 diploma mills doing business in the United States, selling 10,000 to 15,000 phony degree diplomas for fees ranging from a few hundred dollars for a B.A. and up to $5,000 for a doctorate.[3] While the FBI "Operation Dipscam" succeeded in closing down a number of such operations, many survived investigation. Nowadays, a few minutes spent surfing the Web will turn up scores of sites advertising self-styled universities, institutes, and schools that, for payment, will supply college or professional credentials requiring little or no study. Even reputable journals contain advertisements for replacement of "lost" degree diplomas, "second passports," and certificates and licenses of every kind. Despite the efforts made over past decades by federal and state authorities to close down the commerce in deceptive and fraudulent documents, the market continues to operate and is indeed flourishing as never before on a national and international scale.

The abuses perpetrated by rogue organizations should not obscure the fact that many "distance education" programs and correspondence course institutions are highly worthy endeavors, having extremely reputable sponsors. They play a valuable, perhaps indispensable, role in education and training. They are part of the late-twentieth-century burgeoning of nontraditional forms of higher education that developed as a legitimate mode of bringing education to those with limited access to it, typically working people, rural residents, and students with interrupted or unusual educational histories. Awarding study credits for life experience is now a widely accepted practice by both new and long-established legitimate institutions. So is the practice of offering instruction via mail, radio, television, and the Internet. The Open University in Britain, Empire State College in New York State, the Universidad Nacional de Educacion a Distancia in Spain, and the University of South Africa are among those providing top-quality alternatives to conventional ways of acquiring degrees. The University of Buenos Aires, Argentina, has 177,000 students, many enrolled in distance programs, relying on the electronic classroom and support tutorials. Britain's highly respected and pioneer Open University is setting up a subsidiary in the United States (OU-US), which is seeking accreditation, and is collaborating with the State University System of California and the Western Governors Association.[4] But, unfortunately, the advertisements and brochures of the diploma mills, redolent as they are with the rhetoric of "distance learning" and "academic credit for life experience," cast a cloud over the operations of these and many other responsible educational institutions.

Efforts to contain the spread of fraudulent institutions may hinder the work of quite reputable offshore and distance learning schools. In fact, at least one "offshore" medical college, catering in Mexico to U.S. students, has complained that the publicity given to diploma mills may have adversely affected its reputation and that of other schools that, while not at the head of the class, nevertheless offer decent training to students unable to enter more prestigeful schools.[5]

The ordinary employer, let alone the ordinary citizen, can hardly be blamed for harboring uncertainty about which institutions are legitimate and which are scams. The entire picture of higher education in the United States has become blurred, especially in the eyes of employers and students abroad. If there ever was a simple distinction to be made between the conventional college or university, requiring full- or part-time attendance in person, and the outright diploma mill, it is certainly now completely gone. We are witnessing the rapid growth of "no-frills" institutions like the University of Phoenix, which offers its courses in office buildings and business parks to a largely in-employment, adult clientele. Adjunct instructors provide the courses, tailored to the needs of local private and public employers. Already the university is the sixth-largest private university in the United States, boasting an enrollment exceeding 50,000 students on sixty "campuses" in twenty-two states. And it is fully accredited by the North Central Association of Colleges and Schools, one of the six regional accrediting agencies recognized by the U.S. Department of Education.

Though clearly not a diploma mill, the University of Phoenix is no conventional institution of higher learning either.

The vice chancellor of the U.K. Open University advanced this analysis of the challenge to traditional institutions posed by the development of "no-frills" degree programs:

> Today various new providers are moving in to focus exclusively on that kind of teaching. In some jurisdictions, like certain states in the USA, these new suppliers are making inroads into enrolments at existing universities. Because they have a tight focus they do a good job within their frame of reference and have low overheads. Because American universities have been overpriced the newcomers are able to make good profits. Because they had to prise open a market they have been very student-centred, giving students precedence over faculty when it comes to parking and similar revolutionary moves. They have made themselves distinctive. Some of them positively boast about the fact that they are little interested in the nature of knowledge, disinterested enquiry, independent thought and nourishment of teaching by research. But of course they are very eager to gain accreditation as universities and boast about it.
>
> One term for this phenomenon is unbundling. Traditional universities offer a bundle of services; in teaching, research, community involvement, staffing hospitals and the like. Like all organisations offering a bundle of services we cross subsidise between them. All industries suffer upheavals when new providers come along, unbundle a set of services and concentrate on offering the ones that bundled organisations are using as a primary source of subsidy for services that are less financially robust.[6]

An extension of this trend is the so-called cyber-university, essentially an updating of the traditional correspondence course but now offered entirely over the Internet. The first such institution to gain legitimate accreditation is Jones International University, accredited in March 1999 by the North Central Association of Colleges and Schools, one of the six regional accrediting agencies in the United States. Bachelor's and master's degree courses are offered (so far only in applied telecommunications and communications management), at tuition rates averaging $4,000 per year. There is every likelihood that provision of complete courses of study via the Internet will become more commonplace, but along with whatever benefits this may bring there will be an unfortunate downside: doors will be opened wider to organizations less legiti-

mate than Jones International. They will seize on yet another opportunity to offer their dubious wares to a clientele here and
abroad that is either naively ignorant or willfully ready to engage
in academic fraud.

All over the world people have been duped into purchasing fake
credentials, U.S. and foreign. For example, an article in a Russian
newspaper, describing the growth of organized crime, refers to an
Uzbek mafia that can put a price on everything, including academic diplomas.[7] The growth of foreign institutions touting business in the lucrative distance education market prompted Hong
Kong's Non-Local Higher and Professional Education (Regulation)
Ordinance of 1997. Government departments and private employers have turned to the Hong Kong Council for Academic Accreditation for help in assessing qualifications granted by dubious institutions based in the United States.

Credentials fraud appears in many guises, representing different
degrees of misconduct. At the pinnacle stands the deception of obtaining diplomas from organizations that are universities only in
name and not at all in character, the so-called diploma mills. The
U.S. Department of Education defines a diploma mill as "an organization that awards degrees without requiring its students to
meet educational standards for such degrees—it either receives
fees from its so-called students on the basis of fraudulent misrepresentation, or it makes it possible for the recipients of its degrees
to perpetrate fraud on the public."

The ready availability of "mail-order" credentials is signaled in
the classified ads of even the most reputable publications. For example, the November 1998 issue of American Airlines's in-flight
magazine, *American Way,* carries advertisements for six "distance
education" institutions. The *Economist* is a highly respectable and
internationally respected weekly news journal published in several
different editions around the world. But inside its covers each
week the reader will find ads like those on the following pages.

The *Economist*'s justification for carrying ads for institutions that
it knows may be suspect (by making false claims of accreditation,
for example) is that it is not the journal's duty to police the mar-
ketplace. However, when advised that some court or regulatory
authority has found against an institution, the journal will drop its
advertising. The *Economist* did just that with Columbia State University after November 1997, when the British Advertising Standards

Authority Limited advised the journal of Columbia State's "illegit-imacy."[8] However, other journals outside Britain are not necessar-ily that protective of their readers' interests. The phrases "Credit for work and life experience" (LaSalle University), "No classroom attendance. Distance learning" (Monticello University), and "De-grees for people who want to be more effective and secure in their jobs or professions" (Pacific Western University) are the red flags that should alert the wary applicant that something very strange is on offer here.

An Internet site, Dipscam, lists what it considers to be the top ten U.S. diploma mills:

1. Columbia State University (Louisiana)
2. LaSalle University (Louisiana)
3. Chadwick University (Alabama)
4. American State University (Hawaii)
5. American International University (Alabama)
6. Columbus University (Louisiana)
7. Monticello University (Kansas)
8. Frederick Taylor University (California)
9. Pacific Western University (Hawaii)
10. City University (California)

The site then adds two more, one in the United States and the other in Britain:

11. Kennedy Western University (Hawaii)
12. Trinity University (Great Britain)

The *Economist* carries advertisements for some of these diploma mills on its Internet site and for others not listed above, too. A par-ticularly intriguing one is for the Consultants Institute. The insti-tute's brochure opens with the exhortation, "BECOME A CERTI-FIED PROFESSIONAL CONSULTANT IN YOUR OWN FIELD," and goes on to inform the inquirer:

> The world-renowned Consultants Institute now offers you the op-portunity to earn the highest accreditation in the consulting profes-sions by introducing its Distance-Learning Program. In just a few weeks, without leaving your home or office, you can qualify to join the ranks of CPCs (Certified Professional Consultants) who are now

earning $250,000 a year. If you are contemplating a full or part-time consulting career, your CPC diploma—recognized globally by clients in every field—will ensure your success. If you are already a successful independent consultant, you will double or triple your revenues by adding the prestigious CPC acronym to your name.

The Consultants Institute was founded and accredited in 1982 by the Ohio State Board of Higher Education. For complete details, contact Kaye St. Claire, Registrar, The Consultants Institute, Dept. 1A, 30466 Prince William Street, Princess Anne, Maryland 21853 USA.

Why, one might ask, would an institute operating out of the state of Maryland be accredited in Ohio? And, anyway, is the claim that the institute was accredited there in 1982 true? If so, is the accreditation still valid, or has it been revoked or lapsed? And what was the institute accredited to do? Inquiry of the Ohio State Board of Higher Education does not seem to be possible, as no agency with exactly that title currently exists in Ohio (though there are agencies called the Board of Education and the Regents).

Nor does the institute unduly burden an applicant with academic or professional requirements:

The requirements are simple and the tuition fee is amazingly low (with a partial-payment option). The written at-home examination consists of 100 questions—true/false and multiple choice. Use the coursebook to guide you in your answers. A passing grade is 65 percent. You may take the test as often as required at no additional cost, thereby assuring you of your graduation and diploma!

The application form quotes $900 as the full tuition fee, in return for which the course book, the written exam, and free initial membership in the American Consultants League are promised. Presumably the diploma will follow in due course.

Loyola State University's catalogue (1996) lists the kinds of "life-learning" experiences for which applicants could gain credit toward a college degree: playing tennis, visiting a museum, hooking a rug, having intensive talks with doctors, eating in exotic restaurants, and watching public television. Highly regarded Loyola University in Chicago sought to restrain Loyola State from using its name and thus misrepresenting itself. In 1997, Loyola State's Executive Director La Fata was sued for consumer fraud, deceptive practices, and violations of the Illinois Academic Degree Act. Ms. La Fata herself was eminently well qualified to establish her business:

She obtained her diploma from Columbia State University, another notorious diploma mill, on which she evidently modeled her own operation![9]

Quickie degrees in divinity, theology, or religion are especially sought after. One incentive is that there can be certain tax advantages to establishing oneself as a member of the clergy. Some diploma mills even specialize in providing "Christian" degrees.[10] Especially reprehensible is the fact that many of these diploma mills target students in foreign countries. The U.S. reputation in higher education attracts ambitious individuals from other countries, some gullible and others opportunistic, to sign up at "universities" with impressive but deceptive names, such as Columbia State University, LaSalle University, Cambridge State University, and Washington University—all titles deliberately constructed to echo those of more famous institutions. Reliance on such credentials misleads all who are unfamiliar with foreign educational systems and institutions. Increasing international migration plus the international commerce in fake credentials means that what was once restricted to a given country (and therefore reasonably easy to deal with) has now grown to global dimensions, with no single employer able to evaluate properly all the credentials presented by a job applicant.

Universities have offices to respond to inquiries of whether a named person has indeed received a particular degree from a particular institution on a specified date. For example, the University of California at Berkeley has a Verification Unit in its Office of the Registrar. But there are still obstacles in the path of the would-be verifier. A multiplicity of diploma formats exists, not only among universities but even within institutions. Designs may vary from school to school, and certificates change format from decade to decade. In addition, registrars often make it difficult to obtain alumni information, citing privacy considerations.

Inquiring whether an institution is accredited is always advisable but cannot be relied on without further inquiry. Diploma mills have been known to lie outright about their accreditation status, saying that "accreditation is being applied for and is in process" or using some such terms as *registered, licensed, state approved,* or *state authorized*—seeking to suggest accreditation without quite using the word.

Inquiring who is doing the accrediting is a logical next step, for accreditation means nothing if the accrediting body is itself a captive organization of the diploma mill. The World Association of Universities and Colleges (WAUC) and the American World University International (AWU) appear (if only from the common words in their titles) to have a suspiciously close relationship. WAUC labels itself "A Global Accreditation Association," offering "nontraditional" educational institutions accreditation from administrative offices in Henderson, Nevada. Its publicity material states that "qualified universities can join W.A.U.C. as members and later apply for accreditation, based on the quality and merit of their instructional programs." AWU of the U.S. Mariana Islands (it is also American World University—without the *International*—of Iowa City, Iowa, and of Honolulu, Hawaii), states that it is accredited by WAUC, thus raising the question, What is such accreditation worth?

American World University's 1999 catalog informs applicants that although its degree programs (bachelor's and graduate) must be completed within twenty-four months, "the student may work as swiftly as possible toward completion by providing the supervising professor with high quality work. . . . Some students successfully reach their goal in months." Moreover, the tuition policy appears to bear some resemblance to the pricing policy of popular Filene's Basement (daily markdowns of prices, as apparel items remain unsold). Although the regular lump-sum tuition fees for bachelor's, master's, and doctorate degrees are $3,150, $3,450, and $3,750, respectively, a flyer included in the 1999 catalog advertises "Special Spring Tuition Discounts." Complete degree programs in any of more than forty majors were offered at a flat rate of $1,650 (bachelor's), $1,850 (master's), and $2,050 (doctorate), until 31 May 1999 only, giving 40 to 45 percent discounts from the regular rates. Only missing was the exhortation to "HURRY! HURRY! HURRY!" In any event, anyone who waited until the summer of 1999 could have taken advantage of the next discount event—a special summer sale that offered even further savings: the bachelor's degree was now available for $1,500, together with similar savings at the higher degree levels! Given that this "quickie, cheapie" institution claims it is accredited by WAUC, so much for the value of its accreditation.

Not only are employers placed in a difficult position trying to verify their employees' credentials. Reports from many countries indicate the depth and breadth of concern in educational circles, too. Fraudulent diplomas pose problems for legitimate educational institutions everywhere. Italian authorities have attempted to take action against the sale of university degrees and the proliferation of false degrees from obscure institutions.[11] At one time, the Italian Ministry of Education issued blacklists of bogus degree mills, but it conceded that little could be done legally to prevent such fraud. German academics, too, have been distressed at the sale of fraudulent diplomas,[12] and South African and Chinese authorities also have complained of bogus and unearned degrees.[13]

Just as investment companies seek to avoid government regulation via offshore registration, so too do some "degree-granting" institutions. In 1993, a Caribbean-based university was investigated for offering unrecognized British degrees.[14] As fraud perpetrated by diploma mills is revealed, the ramifications may spread far and wide. LaSalle University degree holders in Hong Kong feared that their careers would suffer when they learned of the charges of fraud and tax evasion leveled against its founder, Thomas Kirk II, and they sought to form a self-help group.[15]

FORGERY AND FALSIFICATION

The thriving business in "genuine" credentials by fake organizations presents employers and admissions officers with a host of problems. But they also have to contend with a ready supply of faked, tampered, assumed, and even stolen credentials of genuine institutions.

Securing a genuine university's degree certificate (or transcript) by underhand means can be accomplished in any of several ways: resort to a company that specializes in "document reproduction"—in plain language, forgery; bribing an employee in the target university registrar's office; electronic break-in into the registrar's computer-based records; and even physical burglary of the office. As far as forgery is concerned, one expert investigator of the field has observed,

> College or University Diplomas and Degrees—exact replicas are available for any college or university, anywhere in the world, and are available with the corresponding university's color seal and logo for added authenticity. Companies advertise that among others, they maintain a stock of various degrees for Stanford University, Univer-

sity of Alabama, Harvard University, Ohio State, UCLA, USC, University of Maryland, Michigan State, Duke, Pennsylvania State, N.Y.U., Purdue, Wayne State, London, and Oxford. Some of these paper peddlers, for an additional fee, will provide falsely certified copies of college transcripts which correspond with the degree provided. For another fee you can be provided a preprinted envelope, bearing the university's logo, name, and address. For another fee the company will have your replica transcripts mailed in the university's envelope from the same city as the university on a predesignated date. . . . The cost of replica degrees ranges from $15 to $3,500. . . . The only limitations to obtaining exact replicas of any document or identification are one's imagination and what one is willing to pay![16]

Document replicas are typically advertised as being for the "replacement of lost diplomas" or as "novelties" for the purpose of "entertainment or practical jokes." Customers are asked to provide assurances that the items will not be used to certify educational or professional qualifications. Surely it is not overcynical to regard such requirements as invitations to defraud.

A report on the prevalence of forged academic credentials in Hungary is instructive:

Riga Street in Budapest is home to the Hungarian State Language Examination centre. Each year, inside the prison-like building, hundreds of students take the notoriously difficult proficiency tests. The cafes round the corner buzz with the grumbles and complaints of young Hungarians who have failed the tests—so vital for top jobs in Budapest.

But here everything has a price and some Hungarians are taking a short-cut to success. You can buy a driving licence for £50, a false one-year travel pass for £25, but the foreign language certificates will cost you nearly £250 on Budapest's booming black market in false certificates. . . .

Last month an investigation was made at a provincial university after officials noticed an unusually high number of graduates with language certificates—many turned out to be forgeries. Police then ordered an investigation at 89 Hungarian colleges and universities, checking certificates going back to 1993. Gyula Juhasz, vice-president of the State Language Examination Board, said: "We have begun investigations. In one higher education institution we found 23 out of a group of 30 students held forged language certificates." The investigations have also revealed that some students have been paying others to take the exams for them, using false identification.[17]

Contemporary Moscow also harbors a flourishing market in fraudulent credentials, and according to one investigation this does not appear to be a matter of any great moral concern, at least among young Muscovites:

> The findings [of a survey of Moscow teenagers] revealed moral con-fusion in the respondents' judgments concerning the practice of cheating with education documents. Thirty-six percent disapproved of purchasing a school certificate or college/university diploma. A total of 39 percent did not disapprove of people using fraudulent means of advancing up the social ladder, and one out of every four had a hard time stating his position.[18]

A visitor's report from that city indicated that there is a brisk street market in fake and genuine diplomas. As of mid-1999, about $800 would purchase a blank diploma form of a good university. Blank transcript forms cost only about another $50. However, the price of an officially issued diploma, with proper signature and se-rial number, all duly recorded in a university's books, might run as high as $10,000.[19]

But it would be wrong to think that this kind of trade is confined to the former communist countries. Credentials forgery is certainly not limited to any one place or time. Illustrating the pervasiveness of such fraud across different career paths, in 1998 a Chicago news-paper reported that in the space of a few weeks alone, Illinois im-posters exposed included five Chicago area social workers with bogus degrees, a Peoria student charged with doctoring his college transcript, and a woman falsely claiming that she was a qualified accountant. It also cited Central Christian University in Arkansas, which falsely claimed to be accredited.[20]

In Canada during the 1980s, a Dr. Larry James Falls set himself up in a psychology practice on Vancouver Island. He claimed to have a slew of impressive degrees in psychology and clinical psy-chology: a doctoral degree from the University of California at Los Angeles, master's degrees from York University, Toronto, and the University of British Columbia, and two undergraduate degrees from Dalhousie University, Halifax, Nova Scotia. But by 1991, questions about the genuineness of these credentials were being raised in the community in which "Dr." Falls practiced, and in-quiries to the institutions he had named produced responses that did not bear out his claims. Falls was arrested and admitted he had never attended the institutions in question and held none of their degrees. He confessed to having bought the British Columbia degree certificate for $200. Charged with "Uttering a False Document," Falls pleaded guilty and in December 1991 was given a six-month prison sentence, plus two years of probation—perhaps fairly lenient punishment but not atypical in such cases.

Less wholeheartedly fraudulent, and presumably somewhat more common, are attempts to "improve" otherwise genuine transcripts, say, by substituting better grades in place of poorer ones, inserting courses never taken, or deleting failed or incomplete courses entirely. In addition, "a candidate's official final ranking or diploma may be unjustly enhanced by an official of the exam authority . . . by examination board staff."[21]

LEGALITIES

A person's credentials package will include more than educational certificates. There are birth certificates, evidence of citizenship and residence, details of military service and discharge, listings of previous employment, work performed, grants and contracts secured, research undertaken, publications and unpublished materials authored, awards and honors received, and so on. All such details may be falsified or embellished, either trivially or materially:

> What constitutes a CV [curriculum vitae] lie? Recruitment specialists count anything from altering lengths of time spent at individual companies to cover up periods of unemployment to removing a few years off your age. A report from the Association of Search and Selection Consultants says that a quarter of CVs contain white lies or blatant fabrication. . . .
>
> Yet, according to a report by law firm Harper Macleod, a third of all companies do not check whether job candidates are telling the truth about qualifications. And because of data protection laws, employers are not actually allowed to seek confirmation of qualifications or schools attended. "Even if you are caught out, there are unlikely to be legal ramifications," claims Debra Allcock, head of campaigning at the Industrial Society. "So the worst you can generally expect is being given the sack and having to move on."[22]

Where frauds of this type lie on the continuum of dishonesty is impossible to define a priori; each case must be judged on its own demerits and in the context of the purpose for which the falsification took place.

While some of these fraudulent practices are plainly and universally illegal (e.g., acquiring a forged birth certificate or using forged documents to acquire benefits such as employment), many are not. Padding a curriculum vitae with trivial items inflated to be more impressive (for example, listing a two-minute intervention in a discussion at a professional conference as if it were a full-blown presentation, citing a one-paragraph book notice as a "publication," presenting participation on a minor university committee as a larger responsibility than it really was, or reporting registration for a two-week Harvard summer program as "attended Harvard University") is deceptive and therefore reprehensible. It is unprofessional and unworthy. It can also be counterproductive: excessively long CV's arouse suspicion among experienced users of such documents. But it is not illegal. If one is fired from a position, it is no doubt only prudent to either suppress the fact or imply that there was an agreed parting of ways. Again, that is not illegal. Nor in the United States is it illegal for an individual to enroll with a diploma mill here or abroad, pay the required fees, complete the usually trivial "course assignments," and in short order accept delivery of a splendidly impressive diploma ready to frame and display on the den or office wall. However, if an applicant for a job uses a fraudulent credential in the application, that may be an offence.

What may also be illegal, depending on the laws of the state in which a diploma mill is incorporated and/or operating, is making false claims in advertising and in the business of supplying such credentials. While California (since 1991), Illinois, and New York (for many decades) have exercised strict control over degree-granting institutions operating within their borders, a few states (most notably Hawaii, Louisiana, and Utah) are more hospitable to diploma mills.

Whatever the reasons for credentials fraud not being prosecuted with greater energy, little action seems to have followed the five-year FBI investigation, "Operation Dipscam," undertaken during the period 1980 to 1985. In presenting its report, the FBI claimed that about 200 federal employees, some in high positions, hold phony academic or medical degrees. However, this disclosure appeared to have produced little if any follow-up by government agencies. Only the U.S. Postal Service and the Small Business Administration responded to inquiries about follow-up action on employees reported to hold fake credentials.[23]

In those states that have not yet developed specific mechanisms in their higher education sectors to oversee degree-awarding institutions, it is left to consumer affairs agencies to take action against fraudulent claims made by advertisers. But, just as water runs downhill to seek its lowest point, diploma mills move from states tightening controls to states remaining relatively relaxed. In the 1970s, as other jurisdictions introduced controls over diploma mills, Missouri had become one of these more hospitable states. Until the late 1980s, state control remained notably lax in Missouri, and the state was home to at least nine dubious degree-granting institutions. They were all accredited by the International Accrediting Commission for School, Colleges and Theological Seminaries (IAC), a one-man operation whose owner, a Mr. George Reuter, acted as the "Commission." In late 1989, however, the attorney general of Missouri obtained a court injunction barring the IAC from operation in Missouri and also succeeded in severely restricting the activities of the diploma mills it had accredited.

This Missouri success had the usual consequence: The mills skipped state, this time to Wyoming, which by the early 1990s had become host to more than fifty private colleges offering quickie degrees, typically to out-of-state and foreign individuals: "'You could get anything you wanted—a doctorate, a bachelor's or a master's,' said Jim Boreing of the Wyoming Department of Education."[24] In 1994, Wyoming in turn passed laws to force the diploma mills to register with state education authorities and to demonstrate that they were genuine educational institutions and not operating simply as degree merchants.

In another instance, on 28 April 1999, Hawaii's Department of Consumer Affairs obtained a "stipulated judgment" against Pacific Western University (PWU). The judgment was based on PWU's violations of Hawaii's law dealing with unaccredited degree-granting institutions. Among other provisions, it provided that PWU

is hereby permanently enjoined from making any representations to the effect that it is registered with or authorized by the State of Hawaii to confer bachelor, master, and doctoral degrees, and/or award academic degrees . . . [and] from making any representations that utilize the term accreditation, accrediting, or any form thereof in a misleading manner.

In addition, provision was made for refunds of tuition payments to consumers who had relied on PWU's assurances re accreditation, and for a sum of $30,000 to be paid by PWU to the Hawaii Office of Consumer Protection to help cover the latter's costs in the case.[25]

The complex arrangements set up by yet another diploma mill, Fairfax University, are calculated to frustrate official legal action of this kind. Fairfax takes its name from one U.S. location, is registered for business in another, and operates physically from England. Its fine-sounding name derives from the city of Fairfax, Virginia, even though the university has no tangible connection there. Instead, its catalog explains, "The name 'Fairfax' honors an early Anglo-American connection that exemplifies many of the values for which the University stands. Thomas, 6th Baron Fairfax, inherited land in the Colony of Virginia. . . . Lord Fairfax's life illustrates many of the characteristics and objectives that typify non-residential education." But then one finds that Fairfax University is registered for business in Louisiana, while all communications with prospective customers are made from Peterborough, England! "Elusive University" might be a more fitting name.

Currently, action against diploma mills in the United States has moved on to Louisiana, where the attorney general has set his sights on a number of questionable institutions. Two of these are Columbia State University (CSU) in Metairie and the agency that has "accredited" it: a certain International Accrediting Association, a name familiar from Wyoming's experience. Attorney General Richard Ieyoub asked a state court to prevent Ronald Pellar, owner and operator of CSU, from doing business pending a court hearing, citing consumer protection laws. CSU closed in August 1998 after disclosures that typify the ways in which diploma mills commonly market their wares. It offered degrees that could be obtained in as few as twenty-seven days of "coursework" and for as little as $1,695. A "triple combo" of bachelor's, master's, and doctorate degrees could be had for $3,695. The campus pictured in its brochure was of a historic building in New York, and the president listed bore the name of Austen Henry Layard, deceased over 100 years ago. CSU claimed distinguished alumni, including Jonas Salk, until he protested. The founder, Ronald Pellar, had several aliases, was a television hypnotist known as Dr. Dante, and was once briefly married to Lana Turner. He had already been sentenced to sixty-seven months in federal prison for fraud involving a fake trade training school but escaped and is believed to be living in a yacht off the coast of Mexico. Further evidence that, in this instance at least, crime had paid was unearthed by the FBI. They raided the actual site of the operation of CSU in San Clemente, California, where the agency seized about $500,000, which, they claimed, represented the proceeds of just one week's business.[26]

In the United Kingdom, a governmental body oversees the right of institutions to grant degrees. In addition, there exists an Advertising Standards Authority, which rules on complaints of misleading advertising in education, as well as in all commercial areas. The end result of a complaint lodged with the authority about CSU was typical of the mild kind of sanction meted out by the authority. Columbia State was charged with making false accreditation claims, and in its ruling upholding the complaint, the authority stated,

> The advertisers said they had "non-traditional" accreditation from the Council on Postsecondary Accreditation but did not submit evidence for this. They claimed that their degrees were based on a combination of previous education, life experience and a short study course and applicants had to meet certain requirements before being accepted onto the programme. They did not say or show what those requirements were. The Authority considered that the advertisement gave the misleading impression that the University was officially accredited and exaggerated the value of the qualifications it awarded. The Authority asked the advertisers to change the advertisement to make clear their qualifications were not equivalent to a UK degree.[27]

Although Columbia State seems to have closed up shop, it is not possible to say whether it has reappeared, reborn under another name to carry on with its false advertising and sale of quickie "degrees."

Cambridge State University, closed for fraud in the fall of 1998, was another target of Louisiana's attorney general. It, too, offered applicants degrees at three levels. A bachelor's degree carried a fee of $1,995; $5,295 would pay for the triple combo of bachelor's, master's, and doctorate. They could be obtained in ninety days with credits for life experience. According to the university's brochure, information entered on application forms would not be checked, in conformity with the university's "philosophy of mutual trust." The university's address in Shreveport, Louisiana, was a mailbox from which correspondence was forwarded to an office in California.

Business was brisk: The school had mailed over 22,000 items in the previous five months and logged over 10,000 telephone calls between March and May. No one from this CSU appeared in court to argue against the permanent injunction to cease operations, but soon after, Cambridge State changed its address to a mail drop in Honolulu.

LaSalle University, another "distance education" institution, now also located in Louisiana, used to operate in Missouri and was one of those institutions accredited by the IAC before the state chased it out. LaSalle boasts on its Internet website, "75 degree programs and over 1200 courses in areas designed to improve adult students' general knowledge and to serve their career needs. We offer levels of degrees from Associate to Doctorate."

As already noted, LaSalle threw its net right across the world. Hong Kong students were among those from up to sixty countries who handed over thousands of dollars for mail-order degrees from LaSalle. Their predicament (and, as we have noted, the fragility of their "degrees") came to the attention of employers in Hong Kong when it was reported in 1996 that the university's founder, Mr. Thomas Kirk II, had pleaded guilty to U.S. federal charges of fraud and tax evasion. A Hong Kong newspaper estimated that students all over the world had handed over at least $36 million to LaSalle for their worthless credentials. The operation was closed down in July 1996, after its president and other officers were arrested (and the FBI seized $10 million). However, despite legal pressures and constraints, LaSalle has apparently reopened with new officers and embarked on a serious attempt to "remake its troubled image," as one newspaper headline puts it.[28]

LaSalle had problems with its claims of accreditation, but it now claims interim accreditation from the National Association of Private Non-Traditional Schools and Colleges (NAPNSC). The current description of its accreditation status (also available on its Internet website) reads as follows:

LaSalle University has embarked on a rigorous accreditation effort. . . . LaSalle University has completed application to the NAPNSC Accrediting Commission for Candidate status. The application was submitted August 1, 1997, and the required, initial consultation visit by Commission staff members was received on November 11, 1997. We acknowledge a two-calendar-year validity limit of the application from the date of submission, in the event there has been insufficient evidence of LaSalle's due progress. We also acknowledge that the submission of this application, and its acceptance by the Commission office, do not assure achievement of the status applied for. . . .

LaSalle University urges prospective students to exercise caution in accepting claims of accreditation from any and all distance education schools without adequate research. Meaningful accreditation by legitimate and well-respected accrediting agencies is a difficult, costly and time consuming process. Consequently, many distance education institutions have "self-accreditation" or have established their own "independent" accrediting agencies to satisfy their own needs. Please use caution when selecting an institution based solely on their claims of accreditation.

The careful crafting of LaSalle's language about its own accreditation and the importance of accreditation in general is, indeed, worthy of admiration as an exercise in the cunning use of innuendo and as an exhibition of bold impertinence in the face of legal challenges to its continued operation. At this time, it is a moot point whether the "new" LaSalle University will in fact be able to improve its image and achieve some legality, let alone legitimacy. It should, however, be noted that its accrediting agency, the NAP-NSC, has itself been denied recognition seven times by the U.S. Department of Education.[29]

Louisiana's attempts to press forward with its efforts to close down its diploma mills are evidently meeting with some success. But more is needed. An estimated seventeen institutions are not subject to the jurisdiction of Louisiana's Board of Regents because they are registered as "nonprofit agencies." Attorney General Ieyoub is currently drafting legislation to close this legal loophole, which has attracted many questionable operations, including LaSalle, to Louisiana.[30]

Dubious standards and questionable accreditation have extended into other sectors of education and training, beyond self-styled colleges and universities. In 1988, California was described as a world center of fraudulent trade schools.[31] Consequently, the state legislature created the Council for Private Post-Secondary and Vocational Schools to supervise and accredit that previously unsupervised sector. Currently, however, the trade schools are claiming that the council is overly demanding, bureaucratic, and arbitrary in its decisions, and they are lobbying hard to have the council abolished.[32] In addition, subjecting private trade schools to critical scrutiny of their operations and standards may have some unintended policy consequences. Social policy in the United States is increasingly linking unemployment compensation and other social support services to job-training requirements. A similar situation exists in Britain, where government policy is directed toward expanding opportunities for vocational training and qualifications outside the public schools. Providers of such training are threatened with closure if their claims of performance and operations are found to be wanting, thus reducing opportunities for job training just at the time when other policies are raising the demand.

The United States does not have a monopoly on dubious organizations offering inadequate academic services and fraudulent diplomas. In any country, the coincidence of strong demand for credentials with lax governmental supervision and regulation of degree-granting organizations provides favorable conditions for the establishment and continuing prosperity of diploma mills. Postapartheid South Africa provided just such a combination. A host of repressive laws severely curtailing nonwhites' access to education fell away in the early 1990s, releasing a vast demand for education and training qualifications that overwhelmed the existing government-financed postsecondary institutions. In response, hundreds of private universities, colleges, and training institutions were established, while government had no mechanism to protect the public from the many fraudulent organizations that had suddenly appeared on the South African scene. It is estimated that anywhere between 500,000 and one million persons are studying in these new institutions.

The apartheid regime had maintained such close control over all aspects of educational provision that there had been no particular need to set up an adequate system of quality control and accreditation of postsecondary institutions. Provisions of the 1997 Higher Education Act seek to remedy the situation. All private (including foreign) institutions are now required to register with the Department of Education in Pretoria. The cutoff date for registration passed on 31 March 1999. No unregistered organization was permitted to continue operating after the end of 1999. Meanwhile, registered institutions were given two years to satisfy the government that they are financially viable and academically accreditable—otherwise they, too, would be closed down. The legislation obviously sets high targets for cleaning up the South African private educational situation. Whether the regulatory agencies will have the financial and administrative resources to do the job required (especially in as short a time period as two years) remains to be seen.

The development of reproduction technology and electronic communication has widened the scope of credentials fraud, whether it involves the faking of diplomas or the embellishment of transcripts and resumes. Exact reproductions in "living color," the attachment of holographic images and intricate embossing, printing on special paper, and the forging of signatures—all have been made significantly easier to accomplish as reproduction technology has advanced. The growth of the Internet has meant that diploma mills and "document replacers and reproducers" can offer their wares on a global scale at minimal cost. Even more important, they can quickly pull up stakes and move to another cyberspace location whenever challenged by regulators.

Unaccredited, self-styled universities currently capitalizing on the publicity surrounding distance education advertise their wares on the Internet and World Wide Web, luring students to enter their often expensive programs.[33] In 1997, British police investigated an Internet service that was selling phony certificates and degree diplomas for as little as £70 each. The website offered those who had never had the opportunity to obtain postsecondary education a choice of A-level or degree certificates from any institution in any subject, promising that the certificates would be accepted as authentic.[34] And, in 1998, a company named Prestigious Images was stopped from selling fraudulent university diplomas from a website after college officials and trademark lawyers complained of the trade in what were described as "novelty items."[35]

The American Association of Collegiate Registrars and Admissions Officers (AACRAO) wants all those employed in the business of scrutinizing credentials for college and university admission to become cognizant of the threat posed to the integrity of their institutions by fake and tampered credentials. At the AACRAO 1997 Annual Meeting, a session was held entitled "Internal and External Practices to Combat Credential Fraud." The summary report of the session commences with a reference to "the rapidly increasing amount of credential fraud" and goes on to urge members and their staffs to apply a strict definition of an "official transcript," namely, "one that has been received directly from the issuing institution. It must bear the college seal, date, and an appropriate

signature. Transcripts received that do not meet these requirements
. . . should be routinely rejected for any permanent use." Staff must
be alerted to and trained in all the many ways by which credentials
may be false or falsified, noting especially reports of stolen seals
and blank forms from other institutions. The most important message to all staff, the report concludes, is "VERIFY . . . VERIFY . . .
VERIFY." Prospective students as well as admissions officers and
employers are urged to verify that the educational institution in
question has been accredited, not by any agency, but by one recognized by the Council on Higher Education. Other warnings include
checking with the Better Business Bureau and the attorney general's office in the state where the school is operating.

Hawaii is identified above as yet another state currently making
strenuous attempts to close down the many fraudulent organizations issuing fake credentials within its borders. Its Better Business
Bureau lists the following warning signs that will indicate to degree seekers that all is not aboveboard and legitimate:

Mail is received only at a postal box number or at a mail forwarding
service.

Promotional literature contains grammatical and spelling errors,
words in Latin, extravagant or pretentious language, and sample
diplomas.

Degrees can be obtained within a few weeks or months from the
time of enrollment, and back-dating is possible.

Faculty members hold advanced degrees from the diploma mill itself or similar organizations.

The award of academic credit for life experience is the prime
come-on.

The institution lacks accreditation by an accrediting agency recognized by either the Council on Postsecondary Accreditation or the
Secretary of Education.

Words denoting a legal status such as "licensed," "state authorized" or "state-approved" are misused to suggest an equivalence to
accreditation.

Tuition and fees are paid on a degree basis rather than on a per-
semester, per-quarter or per-course basis.

Prospective students are encouraged to "enroll now" before tuition or fees are increased, or they qualify for a "fellowship," "scholarship" or "grant."

The operation has no library.

For good reason, distance education has acquired legitimacy and mushroomed, in both the number of students and the number of institutions providing for them. But at the same time, the problems of determining the standards and legitimacy of institutions offering programs of this kind have also expanded. We have pointed to the growth of nontraditional, "no-frills," and "cyber" institutions as a factor in the difficulties faced by would-be students and employers seeking to evaluate particular credentials. In addition, the traditional universities are rapidly moving to offer their programs "on-line." Does this mean that we face a future in which a relatively few students will enjoy expensive, high-quality college instruction, based on face-to-face encounters between student and teacher, while the majority will have to be satisfied with cheaper "remote" teaching via electronically communicated images? That is the fear of one critic of the entire movement:

> In recent years changes in universities, especially in North America, show that we have entered a new era in higher education, one which is rapidly drawing the halls of academe into the age of automation. Automation—the distribution of digitized course material online, without the participation of professors who develop such material— is often justified as an inevitable part of the new "knowledge-based" society. It is assumed to improve learning and increase wider access. In practice, however, such automation is often coercive in nature— being forced upon professors as well as students—with commercial interests in mind. This paper argues that the trend towards automation of higher education as implemented in North American universities today is a battle between students and professors on one side, and university administrations and companies with "educational products" to sell on the other. It is not a progressive trend towards a new era at all, but a regressive trend, towards the rather old era of mass-production, standardization and purely commercial interests. . . .
>
> In his classic 1959 study of diploma mills for the American Council on Education, Robert Reid described the typical diploma mill as having the following characteristics: "no classrooms," "faculties are often untrained or nonexistent," and "the officers are unethical self-seekers whose qualifications are no better than their offerings." It is an apt description of the digital diploma mills now in the making. Quality higher education will not disappear entirely, but it will soon become the exclusive preserve of the privileged, available only to children of the rich and the powerful. For the rest of us a dismal new

era of higher education has dawned. In ten years, we will look upon the wired remains of our once great democratic higher education system and wonder how we let it happen. That is, unless we decide now not to let it happen.[36]

Only time will tell if this pessimistic view of the future of higher education will be realized in practice. In any event, if this chapter concludes on a note of "advice to the unwary," it is because of the rapid increase in demand for credentials and the advances in technology that make malpractice easier to accomplish and more difficult to detect. Credentials fraud is no longer a local affair. It is worldwide in scope, enlarging the trade in dubious and forged credentials and increasing the difficulties of maintaining supervision and assuring common, adequate educational standards. The era of "cyberschools" has already arrived, but at this point there is no systematic way of controlling the abuses we have described. Unfortunately, even constant vigilance is no sure safeguard, given the need for expert knowledge to detect fraud and the lack of serious penalties to punish it.

NOTES

1. UNESCO, *Statistical Yearbook* (Paris: UNESCO, 1998).
2. "Bogus Diplomas: Phototypes of Diplomas Bought for $455.00 in May, 1880, by a Representative of the 'Philadelphia Record,'" YA Pamphlet Collection, Library of Congress, YA 19026.
3. "Sending Degrees to the Dogs; the FBI Tries to Throw the Book at Burgeoning Diploma Mills," *Time*, 2 April 1984: 90, 123.
4. Sarah Lyall, "The British Are Coming," *New York Times*, Education Life Supplement, 4 April 1999: 29, 38.
5. Debra Beachy, "Although Healthy, Medical School at Guadalajara Feels Effects of Image of Foreign Diploma Mills," *Chronicle of Higher Education*, 22 May 1985: 35–36.
6. Sir John Daniel, "The Contribution of Lifelong Learning to an Equitable and Inclusive Society," Closing Keynote Address, Universities Association for Continuing Education, 31 March 1999, Internet.
7. Sergei Roy, "Killer Cadres and Leaping Lions," *Moscow News*, 5 June 1997: 6.
8. Suzanne Hopkins (of the *Economist*), personal communication, 6 October 1988.

9. Stephanie Zimmerman, "'University' Is Offering Restitution," *Chicago Sun-Times*, 12 March 1997: 20.

10. Steve Levicoff, *Name It and Frame It? New Opportunities in Adult Education and How to Avoid Being Ripped Off by "Christian" Degree Mills*, 3rd ed. (Ambler, Penn.: Institute on Religion and Law, 1993).

11. Paul Bompard, "Degrees Sold for £15,000," *Times Higher Education Supplement*, 16 October 1998: 10; Paul Bompard, "Police Probe Degree Crime," *Times Higher Education Supplement*, 3 January 1997: 8.

12. Jennie Brookman, "Data Bank Bid to Stop PhD Fraud," *Times Higher Education Supplement*, 17 May 1996: 10.

13. Karen MacGregor, "Register Deadline Set to Trap Fly-by-Night Colleges," *Times Higher Education Supplement*, 5 February 1999: 11; Geoffrey Parking, "False Economy in China's Degree Sale," *Times Higher Education Supplement*, 25 March 1994: 11.

14. Simon Targett, "Offshore Degree Probe," *Times Higher Education Supplement*, 26 November 1993: 1.

15. "Graduate Help," *South China Morning Post*, 24 November 1996: 2.

16. Gregg Colton, "Exam Security and High-Tech Cheating," *Bar Examiner* 67 (August 1998): 22–23.

17. Simon Evans, "Forging a Better Future Can End in Prison," *Times Educational Supplement*, 30 August 1996, Internet.

18. T. V. Koveleva and O. K. Stepanova, "Adolescents of a Time of Troubles: On the Problem of the Socialization of Upper-Grade School Students," *Russian Education and Society* 41 (August 1999): 14.

19. Bryon MacWilliams, "Diplomas for Sale on Moscow's Streets: $800 Degrees from Universities Reflect the Corruption of Russian Higher Education," *Chronicle of Higher Education*, 16 July 1999.

20. Adrienne Dell, "Imposters Say: Just Fake It," *Chicago Sun Times*, 11 June 1998: 6.

21. Vincent Greany and Thomas Kellaghan, "The Integrity of Public Examinations in Developing Countries," in H. Goldstein and T. Lewis, eds., *Assessment: Problems, Developments and Statistical Issues* (New York: John Wiley and Sons, 1996), 175.

22. Kate Hilpern, "Secretaries Aren't Telling the Truth on CVs. Not a Good Idea," *Guardian*, 7 June 1999, Internet.

23. "Only Postal Service Taking Disciplinary Action," *San Diego Union-Tribune*, 13 March 1986: A26.

24. "Surprised to Find Diploma Mills in State, Wyoming Cracks Down," *New York Times*, 26 November 1995: 32.

25. Circuit Court of the First Circuit, State of Hawaii, Civil No. 97-4540-11, "Stipulated Permanent Injunction and Final Judgment against Defendant Pacwest (Hawaii) Corporation, DBA Pacific Western University (Hawaii), Inc.," 28 April 1999.

26. "Why Dr. Dante Is Hiding in a Yacht Off the Coast of Mexico," *Irish Times*, 24 November 1998: 50.

27. Advertising Standards Authority (U.K.), "Adjudication, May 1998, Columbia State University," www.asa.org.uk, Internet.

28. Stacey MacGlashan, "LaSalle University Works to Remake Troubled Image," *Times-Picayune*, 26 October 1998: A1.

29. MacGlashan, "LaSalle University Works to Remake Troubled Image," A1.

30. "Judge Orders Phony College Out of State," *Times-Picayune*, 14 August 1998: B2.

31. D. W. Stewart, *Diploma Mills* (New York: American Council on Education, 1988).

32. "A Lesson in Overkill: Foes of Trade School Oversight Want to Abolish Valuable Agency," *Los Angeles Times*, 27 March 1997: B8.

33. Lisa Guernsey, "Is the Internet Becoming a Bonanza for Diploma Mills?" *Chronicle of Higher Education*, 19 December 1997: A22.

34. Phil Baty, "Degrees for Sale on the Internet," *Times Higher Education Supplement*, 28 February 1997: 1.

35. Lisa Guernsey, "Company Shuts Down On-Line Operation Selling Fake Diplomas and Transcripts," *Chronicle of Higher Education*, 22 May 1998: A32.

36. David F. Noble, "Digital Diploma Mills," March 1988, Internet.

Chapter 4

Professional Misconduct

Misconduct: To mismanage. Malfeasance.

Besides teachers' involvement with cheating on tests and exams, educational and research administrators, researchers themselves, and even parents and politicians may be involved in various kinds of education- and research-related misconduct. For example, it is largely professional persons, not amateurs, who write the essays and dissertations that students buy ready-made. Incidents are reported of research workers massaging and even fabricating data to fit their theories. Referees of research proposals have sometimes misappropriated the applicants' ideas and approaches and used them in their own or their protégés' work. Senior researchers regularly put their names on the research reports of their junior colleagues. Plagiarism is a perennial problem for those engaged in editing professional and popular publications. Politicians pass laws compelling children to attend school but then fail to provide sufficient funds for an adequate education. School systems can and do appoint teachers who are not qualified for the teaching they are doing. In so doing, they may well be committing a fraud: The certificates of graduation awarded may deceive employers and admissions officers about the true quality of the education attested to.

All of this makes a dismal catalog of professional misconduct and misdemeanors in education and research. How prevalent is the misconduct? There is no way to fix its extent precisely, but some indication that it is real and probably growing is given by the proliferation of published guidelines and regulations aimed at informing relevant parties of the standards of behavior expected of them. In the following sections we focus on four aspects of professional misconduct: educational policies that promote fraud, taking bribes in higher education, teachers and administrators helping students to cheat and tampering with test papers, and plagiarism and fabrication.

EDUCATIONAL POLICIES ENCOURAGING FRAUD

In the United States, the constitutions of virtually all of the states place the responsibility for public schooling squarely at state level, but state capitals have devolved their responsibility for providing and financing that education to the localities. Local property tax payers typically provide about half the money needed to run the public schools; federal government money covers about 8 percent; and state resources provide the remainder. This heavy reliance on local property taxes to finance the public schools results in significant inequalities among school systems. These inequalities in turn directly affect the resources available to educate children, including most importantly the number and quality of teachers employed.

In New York State in the mid-1990s, for example, there were just under 700 separate school districts. The poorest tenth of those districts spent an average of $8,200 a year on each pupil, while the wealthiest tenth spent $16,850.[1] Poorer districts lose out when it comes to hiring and retaining qualified teachers, so they routinely hire un- and underqualified teachers as substitutes to staff the classrooms, awarding them emergency credentials. Overall in the United States it is estimated that over one-third of academic subject teachers in the public schools possess neither college major nor college minor qualifications in the subjects they are assigned to teach. The proportion of students taught by teachers with no undergraduate degree in the field reflects similar deficiencies: 32 percent of students in math classes, 33 percent of students in biology, 45 percent of students in chemistry, and 68 percent of students in physics classes.[2] School authorities who engage in such hiring practices are perpetrating fraud on children who are being taught by such teachers.

System-wide educational policies have cheated students, families, and taxpayers in another way, too. With only a few exceptions, state governments in the United States have typically failed to mandate sufficiently high standards for graduation from high school. *Sufficiently* in this instance means graduation standards set high enough so that employers hiring high school graduates can be confident that their recruits come to them equipped with adequate verbal and mathematical knowledge and skills, and that colleges can be confident that few of their freshmen will need extensive remedial work if they are to succeed in their regular coursework. Although the past decade has seen a decided push by many states to raise high school graduation standards (as well as standards of achievement in the lower grade levels), they remain for the most part inadequate.

Heavy reliance on local property tax funding for the schools can promote fraud in other ways, too. It is typically difficult for a child residing in one school district to attend a school in another district, even though both districts are in the same state. And, if permission is granted, the receiving district normally charges a significant fee to out-of-district enrollees. Given that school districts and schools vary greatly in perceived or actual quality, parents are tempted to evade restrictions by less-than-honest devices. They will borrow the address of a relative or friend, use a commercial accommodation address, or even invent a wholly fictitious address to qualify their child's attendance in the favored district.

In chapter 1 we note that school districts typically receive funds from federal and state governments to cover some of the extra costs of educating special education students. This policy is abused when administrators assign children to special education classes primarily in order to secure the additional funds, aiming thereby to lighten the local tax burden. Another abuse of special education provision occurs when children are placed in such classes in order to exclude them from regular assessments of school achievement and so make the results reported for the "normal" school population look better.

The past decade has witnessed a crescendo of complaints about the academic and professional quality of new recruits to teaching, not least from state authorities themselves. Well over forty of the fifty states require prospective teachers to pass some state-administered licensing exam. Massachusetts was a relative latecomer to this requirement. Legislation passed in 1993 was implemented only in 1998, when the Massachusetts Department of Education introduced a basic qualifying reading and writing skills test (together with a test in subject matter for the subject in which certification was being sought) for all would-be certificated teachers. In the first administration of the tests in April 1998, 59 percent of the candidates overall failed to reach the passing grade in one or more parts of the exam. Fearing a backlash from the candidates and from school boards across the state, the department promptly adjusted the cut point to one standard deviation lower, thereby reducing the failure rate to 44 percent. The department felt it was merely following standard practice in tailoring the award of credentials to the number of new teachers needed. Now the backlash came from the public and from the acting governor, in particular, who ordered the department to reverse its adjustments and to have failing candidates retake the test after an interval for more preparation. The entire incident demonstrated in stark clarity the willingness of top educational administrators to perpetrate a fraud on the public by arbitrarily dropping standards they themselves had set and validating the entry into the classrooms of persons who had failed to demonstrate appropriate levels of communications skills (reading and writing) and/or subject area knowledge.

Unfortunately, toleration of low standards extends beyond teachers to students, as well. So-called social promotion policies automatically promote students from a lower to the next higher grade year by year, irrespective of whether the basic knowledge and skills of the lower grade have been mastered. Predictably, teaching and learning in the next grade become very problematic for the student and teacher concerned. In the end it leads to the graduation of high school students possessing diplomas that are little more than certificates of attendance. The qualification is debased for all graduates, the high school becomes in part a degree mill, and a fraud is perpetrated on all concerned—students, parents, taxpayers, college admissions officers, and potential employers. In Los Angeles, an ambitious plan to end social promotion was soon abandoned when it was clear that nearly half of all students would be held back. Even when a definite cutoff score on an important test is set and publicly announced in order to raise standards of student performance, school officials are often prepared to change the cutoff score in the face of criticism from students, parents, teachers, or others: "The Massachusetts state board of education recently set a low passing mark on its new statewide graduation exam, feeling that too many kids would drop or fail to earn diplomas if standards were set too high, and reasoning that it can raise the bar later."[3] At least three other states, Virginia, Arizona, and Wisconsin, have similarly beat a retreat.

Local interest in the operation of an area's public schools carries many advantages, but an important drawback is the potential for undermining professional independence. Such independence should not, of course, be total, but school administrators, teachers, and other school staff often experience great difficulty in resisting the demands of special interest groups, either local or national. Thus, many schools in the United States have been forced to teach a version of the theory of evolution ("creationism") that enjoys little or no support among scholars and researchers in biology. School librarians have been forced to remove "offensive" books from their shelves. The demands of competitive team sports may come to overshadow in importance the normal academic programs of the school because local citizen support for the schools is thought to be (and may well be, in fact) contingent on the school's performance in the local regional football, baseball, or hockey league. In acceding to pressures of this kind, educators may be giving too much away, running the risk of shortchanging their students.

Yet another instance of system-wide policies encouraging fraud occurred in New York City. A high school principal inflated her school's enrollment and attendance figures. By reporting additional names and nonexistent classes, she made the school eligible for additional teachers. The false reports were in part made easier by the Board of Education's system of presuming that students were present unless they were actually marked absent. The school benefited by securing additional faculty; and the principal gained early tenure and bettered her professional reputation—until the misconduct was discovered.[4] So, while fraud is committed by persons, and not by policies or systems, it is nevertheless worth remembering that system-wide policies may be the underlying factors driving that individual misconduct—to the varieties of which we now turn.

BRIBERY

In recent years scandals have erupted in Japan as news of bribes taken by university admissions officers have come to light. In chapter 2 we note that bribes had been offered and accepted to secure entrance to medical schools. At Meiji University in the early 1990s, corrupt officials not only took bribes from the wealthy parents of applicants for admission but even arranged for impersonators to take the entrance exams in place of the applicants.

In higher education admissions in the former Soviet Union bribery was commonplace, and there is no reason to suppose that it is not still occurring. Students in Russia and the Ukraine are accustomed to giving their teachers presents, not just "an apple for the teacher" but often more substantial gifts. Mostly these offerings are innocent of any underhand motive, but the practice can and does quite easily slide over into offering gifts in return for favors— better grades, lighter assignments, and other indulgences.

Also in chapter 2 we cite an incident reported in a Russian medical school, where the dean was allegedly known to accept bribes. The need to give a bribe, in this case to facilitate the admission of a Jewish student, was taken as self-evident. The anxious parent of a candidate for admission simply wanted to know how best to approach the dean with a proposition!

China's state exam system has been accused from time to time of a variety of improprieties, among them the taking of bribes by those with privileged access to the test papers, the grading process, or the award of coveted university admission. Given the intense competition for relatively few places in higher education in China, perhaps what is noteworthy is not the fact that such misconduct occurs but, rather, that so little of it gets reported.

Perhaps we do not need to look as far afield as Japan, Russia, or China to find questionable practices. In the United States, a former instructor at North Carolina's Central University was convicted of passing a student in her course in exchange for the gift of a TV set and a video game: "Zoology lecturer, Vande Reed, gave the student a stolen credit card and asked her to buy the merchandise from the store where she worked." The court placed Reed on probation for three years and ordered her to make restitution to the store.[5]

In the United States, too, and especially in the most prestigeful private colleges, two characteristics of the admissions process conspire to raise at least the appearance of bribery. On the one hand, these institutions run highly professional fund-raising activities, targeted especially at alumni, large corporations, and charitable foundations. On the other hand, the colleges' admissions offices have devised point systems based on desirable student characteristics to try to come up with a "fair, unbiased, objective" basis on which to make admission decisions. Applicant characteristics such as academic performance in high school, SAT scores, extracurricular activity, special talent, and parental alumnus/alumna status all earn points toward a positive admission decision. No problem there, perhaps. But what if the point system takes into account family contributions toward the college endowment? Or what if a large gift from the parent of an applicant simply overrides the point system and facilitates a "special admission"? How far can generosity go before it becomes a bribe in return for the admission of a particular student?

HELPING STUDENTS CHEAT

Teachers Cheating

The Education Act of 1988 in Britain signaled an abrupt departure from a century-long tradition in education. Previous central governments had prided themselves on a "hands-off" policy when it came to school curricula and the maintenance of educational standards. The "British way" was to let each local school authority, head teacher, and even each classroom teacher decide what to teach, when to teach it, and whether and how to assess the extent of students' learning. The 1988 act made deep inroads into such local autonomy by providing for a national core curriculum to cover a minimum of 40 percent of total school time, together with a national system of assessment of students' achievement at seven, ten, fourteen, and sixteen years of age.

Initially, implementation of the program of national testing was boycotted by many teachers; in addition, curriculum and logistical difficulties had to be surmounted. But by the late 1990s the change of policy had been largely accepted, and the national assessments now go forward almost routinely. School-based results are published, as are the results of school inspections. Parents are encouraged to choose a school for their child on the basis of information provided about the measured "quality" of the schools in their county. Test results are most important for determining school status. Local schools are placed in direct competition with each other to capture and retain enrollment and, in consequence, budget, buildings, and staff. Principals and teachers have had to learn to live in a quite unfamiliar competitive environment. Some of them responded by resorting to improper conduct.

From the start of the national testing program, there were allegations of improper teacher behavior. Misconduct was facilitated somewhat by initial looseness in arrangements for shipping test materials to schools. The standard practice (until 1998) was to send each school its test packages a week or two before the test date. The packages included not only the question papers but also instructions for administering and proctoring the tests. This gave teachers the green light to open the packages, and some took the opportunity to review the test questions and arrange for pupils to be coached on the topics. It was not long before complaints were being received from parents that the children had been coached before the test on the very material that appeared on the test papers. After some years of denying that the problem was serious or pervasive, the School Curriculum and Assessment Authority changed the procedures: Administrative instructions are now sent separately ahead of the test papers, and the latter arrive at the schools much nearer the date of the tests.

In an environment where neighboring schools are in competition with each other for pupils, one can expect complaints that pupils in other schools are doing review work on questions that look suspiciously like those that eventually appear on the national test. Is this evidence of teachers' misconduct? Not necessarily so. Given a few years experience of the tests and assisted by the syllabus guidelines, many teachers are able to "spot" topics and even actual questions that are likely to appear. One can hardly fault them for preparing their students accordingly; indeed, they might be accused of dereliction of duty if they failed to do so.

Much more serious, of course, is the possibility that competitive pressures lead principals and teachers to help students cheat or even to tamper with the answer sheets before they are sent to be graded. One complaint of misconduct (this one from a teacher) cited the head teacher as standing by ten-year-old test takers and pointing to the correct answers. An inspector who dropped by the school to check that all was in order had to ring the front doorbell to gain entry. During the inspector's presence in the school, the head teacher stopped her assistance to the pupils. But after he left, it was alleged, she looked through the answer sheets and altered incorrect answers wherever possible.

As a result of such complaints, the government's Qualifications and Curriculum Authority (QCA) has instituted unannounced spot checks on schools. The QCA believes that the incidence of misconduct is relatively small. For example, among 1,000 such checks, only twenty-four instances of irregularities were found. Nevertheless, beginning in 1998, as some small additional guarantee of testing integrity, head teachers have been asked to sign a declaration that the tests have been administered fairly and properly.[6]

How much of this should surprise us? Probably not much. Whenever schools and teachers are placed in competition with one another for status and funds, the temptation will arise to cut corners and beat the system. Misconduct of this kind has a long pedigree in England, going back as far as the mid-nineteenth-century system of "payment by results," according to which elementary school teachers were paid in direct proportion to their pupils' performance in answering the visiting school inspector's questions. One favorite tactic used by the teachers was to take up a strategic position behind the inspector. As he put his questions to the class, the teacher would silently signal prompts to the class: "Hands in pockets equals multiplication, hands behind back equals subtraction," and so on. After all, the school's funding and the teacher's own salary depended on how well the class performed![7]

Tampering with Answer Sheets on Standardized Tests

"Good" schools make an important talking point for real estate agents: Houses in such districts tend to command premium prices. Often the decision to buy turns on whether the purchaser is satisfied that the property is situated in a "good" school district. Even without such incentive, some principals simply want to make their schools look good, so they tamper with their students' answer sheets. Or, if they feel they have been unfairly treated in matters of budget or staff, they upgrade their students' scores and rationalize the misconduct as simply a way of redressing the balance.

An incident of this type occurred in 1991 in Lake Forest, Illinois, a high-income Chicago suburb, where third graders scored very high on a standardized test. Seven teachers claimed that they were pressured to prompt students with answers to the test questions and even to accept subsequent tampering with the answer papers. After investigation, the principal was suspended.[8] A more widely noted incident occurred in the mid-1990s. Streatfield School in Fairfield, Connecticut, was renowned as a "superior" elementary school, its excellence testified to by the consistently high scores of its students on standardized achievement tests. But by 1996 suspicion was raised that someone, perhaps the Fairfield superintendent of schools or perhaps the school principal, Mr. Roger Previs, had tampered with the answer sheets. Local and national press gave much publicity to this case, and a state investigation was ordered. In the end, the investigators were unable to link the principal positively to the tampering but concluded that he was the only person who could have done it. The Fairfield school board began proceedings to dismiss him, and the principal took the opportunity to retire.[9]

Similarly, in 1998 in Brooklyn, New York, it was revealed that a high school principal had padded students' grades, had instituted classes in which students were not expected to do any work, and had revised failing Regents' (high school leaving) exams. Many students who were not entitled by their performance to receive diplomas had received them.[10]

The following year, the New York City school system was hit by a parallel, but now much wider, scandal. In December 1999, the system's special investigator issued a report citing the names of forty-seven teachers and principals in eighteen of New York City's thirty-three school districts who had helped their students cheat on standardized achievement tests. Teachers were alleged to have had their students note their answers first on plain paper, and they would then assist them in correcting errors before they entered their answers on the official answer sheets; or they would have the students correct errors directly on the answer sheets. Apparently some 1,000 test papers were compromised. At least nine teachers were dismissed, and many more were reassigned. One thousand suspect answer sheets is not perhaps an intolerable number in a school system that enrolls roughly one million students, but it is certainly a further signal that some of New York City's school districts continue to be plagued by corruption and misconduct. There is every likelihood, too, that such misconduct will become more frequent, as the school board and New York State place ever greater emphasis on raising achievement test scores.[11]

While the misconduct in New York City's schools occurred mostly in the more disadvantaged districts, the Massachusetts Department of Education has been concerned that teachers in some of the most prestigious schools were helping their students to cheat on the tests given as part of the Massachusetts Comprehensive Assessment System (MCAS). "At least eight teachers were reprimanded or suspended for improper administration of the tests," according to the *New York Times*. The same article quotes a researcher at Boston College's Center for the Study of Teaching as prophesying, "This is just the tip of the iceberg of what's going to happen as the stakes relating to the MCAS test get higher and higher."[12]

A recent example of misconduct reaching further up the administrative hierarchy than cases in Fairfield or New York City came to light in Austin, Texas. In April 1999, a grand jury handed down sixteen separate indictments against the city's school system and its deputy school superintendent for manipulating the district's results on the Texas Assessment of Academic Skills. The results are used to gauge the performance of schools and students. In this incident there was no tampering with students' answer sheets. Instead, ID numbers of low-scoring students were changed so that their scores were automatically discarded by the computer program used to collate results. This had the effect of raising the district's average reported scores. Moreover, misconduct in the Texas testing program is not confined to Austin. Other school districts have apparently had their problems, including an allegation against a principal and a teacher who resigned during an investigation in the Fort Bend School District.[13]

Because of their high-stakes athletics programs, American universities are especially vulnerable to misconduct by professionals. In many institutions, athletes are recruited for their abilities on the sports field, seemingly without regard for their academic qualifications. Despite attempts to help such students, low graduation rates embarrass large institutions that depend on the success of their sports teams for millions of dollars of income. The University of Minnesota earns vast sums for television rights and merchandising and has been plagued by seven scandals connected to its sports programs since the 1970s, including payoffs to players, embezzlement, and sex abuse charges. Most recently, an employee in its athletics department completed over 100 assignments for as many as twenty basketball players to ensure that they maintained their academic standing and could continue to compete. Upon investigation, the employee was sacked, several players were suspended, and the university president observed that evidence revealed "massive cheating and a general attitude of hear-no-evil, see-no evil." And all of this despite the rules of the NCAA, the body that governs most intercollegiate sports in the United States.[14]

Tricking the School Inspectors

Since 1992, Britain has entirely revamped its system of school inspections in order to ensure that every school is inspected for the quality of its education within a space of four years and at regular intervals thereafter. The reconstruction of the school inspectorate played a central role in achieving the British government's goal of providing parents and taxpayers with more (and more reliable) information about the quality of the education given in each school. Inspectors' reports not only highlight the strengths and weaknesses of individual schools but also identify teachers who are failing to do a satisfactory job. How reliable are the reports?

Early in 1998 a member of the Labour Party's task force on educational standards identified fifteen ways in which some heads of schools were attempting to trick inspectors, hoping thereby to improve their schools' images. Among them were:

- keeping troublesome pupils at home for the week of the inspection;
- "papering" the school's correspondence file with congratulatory letters solicited from parents, while suppressing complaints;
- insuring that off-beat, unkempt, or unattractive teachers were not in school that week, having been sent off on a course or a school journey, or having called in sick;
- using bribes and rewards to insure everyone behaves well during the inspection;
- repeating lessons that have gone well in the past;
- calling in consultants to advise on what changes should be made to impress the inspectors;
- arranging "dress rehearsals," often with the consultants acting the role of inspectors.[15]

Such tactics undermine the spirit of the inspection system and tend to defeat its goal of providing reliable public information about the quality of the education provided by schools. Against this, it could be argued that, while head teachers may not be playing the game wholly according to rule, they are not perpetrating an outright fraud. Rather, many of the gambits could be defended as simply a head teacher's effort to show the school in the best possible light. More to the point, perhaps, is the question of how far they do in fact fool the inspectors—something that depends largely on the acuity of the inspecting team, especially its leadership. Although it is reasonable to assume that some trickery goes on, a lot of it is presumably detected and discounted. In any event, a single change in procedure would help deal with the problem. At present, schools are given long notice of an inspection, thus providing the opportunity to plan and execute deceptive tactics. Much shorter notice periods (one week, for example) would do much to discourage them.

Undermining Standards in Vocational Training

Vocational training establishments in both the United States and the United Kingdom have been subjected to allegations of professional misconduct. In both countries, funding for vocational training institutions has been based on the number of credentials they award. In addition, many of these credentials are not awarded on the basis of an external assessment of students' knowledge and skills. If assessment is done internally by the teachers themselves, we should not be surprised that the system carries with it both incentive and opportunity to lower standards.

In the 1990s, Britain introduced a new system of National Vocational Qualifications (NVQ). The aim was to systematize such qualifications and provide a ladder of increasing knowledge, achievement, and skill, together with associated credentials. It was hoped that this would help to place vocational education and training on a par with the traditional and highly esteemed academic qualification, the Advanced Level General Certificate of Education (A-level).

By 1994, criticism of assessment practices among providers of training (technical colleges and private providers) had become a subject of public discussion. It was alleged that achievement standards had fallen because the system was basically flawed: Colleges and providers were permitted to assess their own students, without any external tests or exams, while at the same time their funding was partly tied to the number of students they enrolled and the number they graduated. A report from the National Institute for Economic and Social Research concluded that credentials could not be trusted when payment was dependent on outcomes.[16] In 1996, the National Audit Office investigated allegations of misconduct by vocational training institutions. Its report noted that unscrupulous operators put in claims well before students had completed their programs, as well as when students had not met minimum attendance requirements, and had even forged certificates in order to claim payment under the government's program.[17]

In 1999, a court case revealed further fraud possibilities in the area of training for NVQ credentials. Link Training, a private provider of training services for the NVQ, worked under contract for the North Derbyshire Tertiary College, Chesterfield. It supervised the practical training of youngsters enrolled in the college in firms around the country. Link complained that the college had refused to pay its bills (£3 million) for services rendered. The college justified its refusal by pointing to evidence that Link was submitting fraudulent bills and cited instances of claims that could only be fraudulent. For example, Link had claimed for eighty hours of work in one day by a single woman tutor, who was supposed to be supervising thirty-five students in ten different workplaces; another claim was for seventy-four hours of work in a single day by one tutor. The Serious Fraud Office has announced that it will conduct an investigation of Link's practices. Left-wing critics have long criticized the practice of contracting out to the private sector training for government credentials such as the NVQ certificate. Anthony Wedgwood Benn, MP, one such critic, has charged that the system of private provision of vocational training inevitably leads to corruption and to the debasement of standards for the NVQ.[18]

Cash Bonuses and Teacher Misconduct

Additional evidence that cash bonuses for scholastic improvement will evince similar allegations of teacher misconduct comes from Kentucky. Beginning in the early 1990s, a statewide school reform movement provided for cash bonuses directly to teachers whose students improved their academic performance. Many teachers responded by "allowing students to use textbooks to find test answers, edit[ing] essays before they were written in the test booklet and giv[ing] out questions in advance," as well as deliberately miscalculating and inflating the grades they awarded on portfolios of student work. In 1993, a state audit found that teachers at 96 percent of the audited schools had inflated portfolio grades by an average 35 points on a scale of 140. One elementary school jumped from below average to become one of the highest scoring in the state, as teachers at the school complained that their colleagues had been inflating portfolio grades.[19]

The Lake Wobegone Effect

In 1987, John J. Cannell published studies of the relationship between national educational norms on the major standardized achievement tests (California, Iowa, Stanford, and so on) and the scores on those tests reported by the fifty U.S. states. His analysis reveals that all fifty states were reporting test results above the publishers' national norms. He called this "the Lake Wobegone effect," in reference to the fictional radio show town, where all the children are above average. A resurvey in 1989 found that forty-eight of the states were testing above the national norms, while 90 percent of the elementary schools and 80 percent of the secondary schools were doing so. What might be producing such remarkable results?

Among the many possibilities, Cannell cited cheating by students, deceptive testing practices (such as excluding known poor achievers from taking the test), and misleading reporting methods. Pressure on school superintendents, principals, and teachers to demonstrate that their schools produce tangible results in the form of high test scores was cited as a standing incentive to manipulate and fudge.[20]

Model Answers and Parroting

Hundreds of Hong Kong high school seniors were penalized in their 1996 A-level Chinese language exam for repeating verbatim parts of model answers provided by coaching schools. The exam requires students to write short compositions in Chinese on fairly obvious topics, some of which tend to be repeated year after year.

The coaching schools "spot" these topics and provide model compositions for the students to memorize. The examiners refused to award marks for passages in compositions that appeared to be parroted back from model answers. They lowered the grades of 152 students for this reason, of whom 118 failed, although seven of these were subsequently upgraded on appeal. All of this led to a storm of protest from the public, much of it in favor of the students.[21]

Situations of this kind raise the question, How far should teachers go in supplying model answers to questions likely to appear on the question paper? Also, if all they do is parrot back the text of the model answer, are students learning anything valuable? Are teachers cheating their students and behaving unprofessionally? Certainly in the United States most observers would severely criticize such practices. But what if in a given school system rote learning is standard practice, as it is in many countries around the world? In any case, where is the line between acceptable and unacceptable practice to be drawn? Is it OK for the teacher to drum into the students' heads, say, five points to hit on the exam should the examiners ask, "What factors led to the outbreak of World War II in Europe in 1939?"; but is it not OK for the teacher to provide the verbatim text of an answer that could be written out by candidates in the fifteen to twenty minutes they have to respond to a question?

Tutoring and Coursework

In many countries, and not just the richer ones, out-of-school coaching, private lessons, and summer tutoring have become well-established practices. As students approach high-stakes exams toward the end of their secondary school careers, parents are willing to pay for the extra help that may well give their son or daughter an advantage in the competition for a place at the next level of education.

The past decade has seen a movement to expand assessment practices (especially at the secondary school level) from the traditional mode of closed book, time-limited, and proctored hall exam toward including grades given during regular coursework and homework and grades on "portfolios" of students' assembled work. The twin rationales for change are that only a relatively narrow range of student performance can be captured by traditionally organized exams and that wider programs will enable a wider range of skills and knowledge to be assessed. The downside is a loss of security in the assessment process: There is a greater chance that students will be presenting the work of relatives, friends, tutors, coaches, or even commercial suppliers rather than their own unaided efforts.

In England, most of the grades on the exams for the General Certificate of Secondary Education (GCSE), usually taken at age sixteen, are based on the results of exam answers, but in some subjects part of the final grade is derived from a teacher's grades on the candidate's coursework and independent assignments. When coaches and tutors are asked to give help on these assignments, they are placed in an invidious position. As the organizer of a tutoring service has observed, "It is one thing to offer advice and constructive criticism—in other words, to teach: It is another to be a surrogate candidate." For example, a tutor prepared her tutee with a complete set of responses to a foreign language oral exam.[22] Although this instance occurred in 1990, the problem has hardly disappeared and has spread from the lower level exam (the GCSE) to the pre-university A-level exam usually taken at about age eighteen. Under the guise of requesting instruction on a topic, students are really asking for help in answering specific homework/coursework assignments. Nowadays, too, access to help is facilitated by sophisticated communications technology: cell phones, fax, and e-mail messaging. Cell phones now come equipped with Internet and e-mail capabilities, making it easier than ever for students to cheat on their homework tasks and on tests. Nor are these devices beyond the financial reach of many children. In Britain, pre-Christmas sales of mobile phones to children were estimated to have reached 300,000. Market surveys have shown that these phones are now what children most want as a present, handily beating even computer games.[23]

Commenting on this phenomenon, Robin Bennett, managing director of London Tutors, has estimated that up to one-quarter of all calls to his tutors are from tutees looking for help with their course assignments. His agency has banned tutors from helping students with their coursework assignments—but other agencies are not so fastidious: "Many of them [tutees] don't even seem to think they are cheating. It is unfair to the other students and to the tutor involved."[24]

This kind of problem now seems to be spreading rapidly into higher education. Increasingly, there are reports of tutors writing essays for university students for a fee, currently in the neighborhood of £300. Foreign students are these "tutors'" most frequent clients, as they have to find some way around their poor English language skills.[25]

PLAGIARISM

In the past, "borrowing" other composers' themes was almost standard practice in music—and was certainly done without any thought or necessity to acknowledge the provenance. Today's saturation of the audio environment with recorded and live music of every genre renders some amount of unwitting copying almost inevitable. Whether a given instance of replication rises to the level of copying, and then to the additional level of plagiarism, often falls to the lawyers to haggle over and the courts to decide.

Incidents of plagiarism occur constantly in all kinds of creative work: musical composition, writing, the graphic arts, and so forth. Perhaps to have one's work copied can be regarded as the highest form of flattery, but plagiarism is not just copying. It is deliberate, witting copying without acknowledgment, typically nowadays not something welcomed by the original creator.

It is useful to distinguish among degrees of copying: There is unwitting, "arm's-length" replication (I simply reinvent someone else's text, tune, or design without ever having had access to the earlier version); then there is unconscious or negligent copying (I simply forgot that I had prior knowledge of the original and recreated it, thinking all the time that it was my own invention—and so omitted acknowledgment of the original); and last, there is intentional copying (in which I deliberately pass off someone else's work as my own, knowing full well where it came from). The greatest danger to writers, scholars, composers, and so on is unconscious or negligent copying, which can easily occur when a work takes years to complete. Over time, memory fades of just where that research note, that scrap of musical notation, or that jotted down aphorism or idea came from. Few authors are careful enough to document the source of every single note they make in preparation for their writing. Therein probably lies the source of most alleged plagiarism. In any event, we recognize that all "new" ideas derive from a background of "old" ones. If we are all "pygmies standing on the shoulders of Newton," dependence on the work and ideas of others is inevitable.

An example of what appears to have been deliberate plagiarism surfaced in mid-1998. When John Wiley and Sons published James Mackay's *Alexander Graham Bell: A Life*, the book was favorably reviewed. The *New York Times* called it "compelling." But then, Robert V. Bruce, a Boston University emeritus professor, wrote to the publisher pointing out that Mackay's book followed very closely (he believed much too closely) his own 1973 book, *Bell: Alexander Graham Bell and the Conquest of Solitude*. Bruce identified many passages in the new book as virtually verbatim extracts from the 1973 biography. Most damning were Mackay's acknowledgments and thanks to the National Geographic Society for allowing him to use the materials they held on the inventor in "the Bell Room." But the society's Bell Room ceased to exist a couple of decades previously when its holdings were transferred to the Library of Congress. In the 1973 book Bruce cites the Bell Room in his acknowledgments, so it is most probable that Mackay could not have seen the sources, except as they were presented in Bruce's book. In 1998, John Wiley and Sons, Mackay's publisher, withdrew the book and destroyed its stock of copies. At least four of Mackay's recent books have been questioned as plagiarized in part, but that does not appear to have caused him to stop offering additional manuscripts to publishers—or publishers to stop accepting them. In 1999, Atlantic Monthly Press was about to publish his "new" life of John Paul Jones, the American naval figure, when allegations of Mackay's substantial plagiarism of an earlier biography of Jones by Samuel Eliot Morison caused the press to halt sales. Mackay is adamant that he has not plagiarized other authors and vows to keep on writing books, adding to the over 100 volumes that already bear his name.[26]

From biographies to textbooks, plagiarism turns up only too often. In 1975, a federal district court judge handed down a judgment that led to what was at that date a record figure of damages awarded against a publisher for producing and distributing a plagiarized work. The case involved the Meredith Company, publisher of a textbook entitled *Child Psychology*. Professor Brian Sutton-Smith, a well-known scholar in the field, was listed as the author, although the book was known in the trade as a "managed" book. This indicated that the manuscript for the book had not been written by the listed author but, rather, by a team of scribes, guided to a greater or lesser extent by the professor. This practice is by no means unknown, especially on the textbook side of publishing.

Soon after publication, Harper and Row sought an injunction to bar Meredith from continuing to sell its book, on the ground that substantial sections were plagiarized from Harper and Row's book by authors Mussen, Conger, and Kagan entitled *Child Development and Personality*. During the court proceedings it became clear that the listed author had deliberately guided his scribes to follow the general structure of the Harper and Row book, as well as urging them to appropriate specific passages (although there was also some contradictory evidence that in the early stages of book preparation he had objected to what he viewed as the publisher wanting to follow too closely the outline of the Harper and Row book). In the end, the judge did not mince words in finding decisively against Meredith and the author:

> Perhaps one-third or more of the Meredith book is, in my opinion, a recognizable paraphrase of Mussen, third edition. . . . In sum, I conclude that Professor Sutton-Smith was fully aware of the proposed method of preparation of the Meredith text and the direct use which was in fact made of Mussen as to both content and sequence. I conclude that he not only acquiesced but also participated in its being prepared in that fashion, seeking only to prevent blatant similarities.[27]

Another instance of scholarly plagiarism occurred also in the 1970s, though it was not brought to light until the 1990s. Bruno Bettelheim, who came to the United States from Austria just before the beginning of World War II, quickly made a name for himself as a child psychologist with particular expertise in dealing with autism among children. He built a stellar career at the University of Chicago and in 1976 published his best-selling book, *The Uses of Enchantment: The Meaning and Importance of Fairy Tales*. The book focuses on the tales of the Brothers Grimm, and Bettelheim argues that over the centuries the telling and retelling of the same folk stories led to refinement of their details to produce the Grimms' polished versions. Of course, critics quickly pointed out that the Bros. Grimm had themselves faked and prettied up their stories in one inspired rush in the early 1800s, an inconvenient fact that Bettelheim had overlooked and which exploded a landmine under his argument. However, Bettelheim would not have been the first author to have his book thesis laid low by critics pointing to contradictory facts. But there was much worse to come.

Bettelheim died in 1990, and in 1991 Alan Dundes, a noted folklore scholar, announced that *The Uses of Enchantment* contained substantial portions of copied (and unattributed material) from a 1963 volume, *A Psychiatric Study of Myths and Fairy Tales: Their Origin, Meaning and Usefulness* by Julius E. Heuscher.[28] Another author, Richard Pollak, followed this with his book, *The Creation of Dr. B*, in which he details the results of his investigation of Bettelheim's claims about his life in Europe and his work in the United States. Pollak was able to produce a mass of evidence that Bettelheim had played fast and loose with the truth in many ways. Pollak demonstrates that, far from the plagiarism contained in *The Uses of Enchantment* being an isolated event in Bettelheim's scholarly career, the fact was that he had invented a whole new persona for himself after arriving in the United States in 1939. In addition, Pollak provides detailed evidence that Bettelheim had falsified very important elements in reports of his clinical work, drawing much more on his imagination than his experience.[29]

Another form of plagiarism occurs when senior researchers and scholars put their names on the published works of their juniors and assistants, without acknowledging the full extent of the latters' contributions. The practice is widespread in the reporting of scientific and technical research and can perhaps be justified when the research has been done in the senior researcher's laboratory, using funds he or she has acquired. One of the most extraordinary allegations of a "senior" denying an associated researcher due recognition has to do with the authorship of a number of Albert Einstein's most significant scientific papers in the first decade of the twentieth century—papers that placed his name in the pantheon of modern physics. The allegation surfaced after 1986, when Einstein's love letters to his first wife, Mileva, were published.[30] In them he wrote of her doing his mathematical work for him and of how she was his intellectual equal. Yet, perhaps because of the strong prejudice against women in science, Einstein's name alone appeared on his early papers, with no acknowledgment of the important contributions most probably made by Mileva.

FABRICATION

The record of scientific research is littered with instances of fabrication of research results, whether it's the complete and outright
invention of fake experiments and their alleged results; the high-
lighting of supporting evidence and the suppression of counter-
evidence; or the statistical "massaging" of data to produce a desired conclusion. Even Isaac Newton indulged in unpardonable
professional misconduct during his long-running and bitter dispute with Leibnitz over who was entitled to priority for the invention of the calculus. As president of the Royal Society, Newton
packed a committee of inquiry into the dispute with his favorites
and supporters, directed the inquiry himself, made sure its conclusions favored his own claim, wrote the committee's final report
anonymously, and topped everything off by anonymously publishing an anonymous review praising his own anonymous report![31]

In our own time, the founding director of the FBI, J. Edgar
Hoover, was the consummate bureaucrat, ever alert for opportunities to expand his organization's sphere of activity and reputation.
A major part of that reputation was built on the alleged prowess of
the FBI Crime Laboratory. Recently evidence has accumulated re-
vealing a disturbing degree of misconduct in the lab's work: sloppy
handling of evidence, doctored reports, errors in testimony, sub-
standard analysis, and poor practices at various important laboratory units. The consequences of reporting faulty and/or faked research results in serious criminal cases are so grave (false
convictions and imprisonment, perhaps even executions) that one
can only wonder at the degree of inhuman indifference to suffering
shown by the technicians and executives who engaged in the reported misconduct.[32]

An organization of editors of medical journals in Britain, the
Committee on Publication Ethics (COPE), had this to say about
research fraud: "Research integrity spans study design, collection and collation of results, and data analysis and presentation.
Failure amounts to errors of judgment, to 'trimming and cook-
ing,' through to blatant fraud."[33] An extensive literature bears
witness to the nature and frequency of such fabrications. A few
titles taken from a list of many hundreds are S. Lock and F. Wells,
eds., *Fraud and Misconduct in Medical Research* (1996); Daniel J.

Kevles, *The Baltimore Case: A Trial of Politics, Science, and Character* (1998); Robert Bell, *Impure Science: Fraud, Compromise and Political Influence in Scientific Research* (1992); David J. Miller and Michael Hersen, eds., *Research Fraud in the Behavioral and Biomedical Sciences* (1992); *Scientific Fraud: Hearings before the Subcommittee on Oversight and Investigations of the Committee on Energy and Commerce, House of Representatives, One Hundred Second Congress, First Session, on Apparent Wrongdoing at the NIH Laboratory of Tumor Cell Biology and Actions Involving the Office of Scientific Integrity* (6 March and 1 August 1991).[34]

We note above the possibility that many instances of plagiarism are unconscious and unwitting on the part of the copier. It is a little more difficult to understand how this can happen with the fabrication of research results, but nevertheless researchers, like other human beings, are quite capable of reporting only the things they want to see and of ignoring any contrary evidence, especially if what they think they have seen fits in with their theoretical preconceptions.

This is what may have happened to a noted educational research psychologist, Cyril Burt, in England. In a long and illustrious career, he bestrode the world of research psychology as a professor at University College London, knighted by the king, and recipient shortly before his death of the Edward Lee Thorndike Award of the American Psychological Association. His commanding presence, rhetorical skills, readiness to draw important policy conclusions and recommendations from his results, and sheer longevity (he lived until age eighty-eight) all came together to place him alongside such giants as William James and E. L. Thorndike. His scholarly work centered on analysis of individual and group differences in "intelligence," primarily as measured by conventional IQ tests given to sets of twin children. One major conclusion he drew from his results was that IQ differences are largely genetic in origin. If, as he found, IQ scores among children of poor families were lower than the scores of children from wealthy families, the difference was to be ascribed to poor genes, rather than poor environment. His conclusions fit well with prevailing prejudices among the British public and supported the so-called tripartite structure of public education. This provided for selection by exam at age eleven for either academic secondary schools (continuing to age sixteen or eighteen) for the talented 15–20 percent; or for elementary schooling (ending at fourteen or fifteen years of age) for the mass of youngsters; or for a few vocational schools for the in-betweens.

Within a year of his death, doubts about the integrity of his research began to be published. Critics asserted that two of Burt's fieldworkers did not in fact exist or, if they did exist, they could not have done the data collection and analysis Burt ascribed to them. There was reason to believe that the articles and reviews they were supposed to have authored were written by Burt himself, using their names as pseudonyms, and were published in the journal of which he had been the longtime editor. This was followed by allegations that statistics cited by Burt were suspiciously identical (from what at first sight appeared to be three different samples of identical twins) and suspiciously exact (carried to three decimal places). A heated debate ensued between these critics and the defenders of Burt's very high reputation, ending in victory for neither side. The initial suspicions that Burt had played fast and loose with reasonable research and publication protocols were not allayed. Nor is the mystery likely to be definitively solved. Burt was not a careful archivist of his research materials, keeping them stored en masse. Much of it was destroyed, some during wartime bombing, some after his death. As one critic (Robert Joynson) of the attacks on Burt's reputation has concluded, "The precise apportionment of praise and blame in the case of Cyril Burt may well have to be left to the day of judgment, when it will provide a severe test of the infallibility of the Almighty."[35]

MEDICAL RESEARCH

Burt's misconduct, if such it was, occurred more than fifty years ago. But today's researchers are probably at greater risk of committing research fraud. In the United States, about 3,000 institutions receive federal government research grants. The government's Office of Research Integrity receives thirty-five to forty notifications a year of investigations of alleged misconduct in research, of which the office makes about fifteen positive findings annually.

In 1997, the *British Medical Journal* carried the following report:

John Anderton, a consultant physician in Edinburgh and former registrar and secretary of the Royal College of Physicians of Edinburgh, was struck off by the General Medical Council (GMC), which regulates medical practitioners in Britain, for faking data in a clinical trial. The misconduct came to light because of an investigation by a pharmaceutical company, Pfizer, for which he was conducting the research. The company was helped by the private agency set up to investigate possible cases of research misconduct that is associated with Frank Wells, former medical director of the Association of the British Pharmaceutical Industry. Dr. Wells, a coauthor of the BMJ Publishing Group's book, *Fraud and Misconduct in Medical Research*, says that his agency is constantly busy. Its main customers are pharmaceutical companies and health authorities. Since 1989 Dr. Wells has reported 17 cases to the GMC, all of which have resulted in findings of serious professional misconduct. The agency has another 12 cases pending.[36]

Also in Britain, the editors of medical journals who have organized themselves into the watchdog and action committee COPE have observed:

In the UK many of the cases involve fabrication of the clinical trial data, mostly by general practitioners, although hospital clinicians have been guilty of similar offences. Fraud in laboratories seems to be less of a problem, although there have been some notorious cases in the USA and the UK.

William Summerlin, an immunologist at the Sloane-Kettering Institute in New York, is the man credited with starting research misconduct, as we have come to know it. In 1974 he used a black felt tip pen to colour patches of transplanted skin in white mice. Others have claimed that isolated cell lines came from human diseases, when subsequent work proved that these had come from a monkey. The examples are legion.[37]

In two years of operation up to 1999, COPE investigated sixty cases of possible misconduct, which included five incidents of data falsification or fabrication. Some professionals oppose COPE's work, arguing that the editors are exaggerating the problem of misconduct and citing the relatively small number of serious incidents in support. COPE's response has been that it is important to demonstrate that misconduct in research and publication, however rare, is not being ignored.

The organization's point was soon underlined by what happened at a meeting of the American Society for Clinical Oncology in May 1999. Dr. Werner Bezwoda, an expert in chemotherapy holding the chair in medical oncology and clinical hematology at the University of the Witwatersrand, South Africa, presented startling results of his research on the treatment of breast cancer. He reported that combining bone transplants with massive doses of chemotherapy (as much as twenty times normal amounts) had produced excellent positive results in trials on 154 women with advanced breast cancer. Because this result flew in the face of much medical opinion and of four other studies presented at the meeting, the society sent out a team to Johannesburg to review his research protocols and data. It became clear that Dr. Bezwoda was not able to produce records for even half of the number of women he claimed to have treated, that he had not obtained the patients' informed consent, and that some substantial portion of his results might well have been fabricated. By the end of January 2000, Dr. Bezwoda had admitted to serious misconduct in his research and had resigned his university position. His parallel position with the provincial health authority was placed under threat.[38] A system that relied primarily on the professional integrity of its research personnel had spectacularly failed to justify its trust. The message was clear: In matters of medical research and publication, eternal vigilance was a requirement, not an option.

Why a researcher fabricates favorable research results or suppresses unwelcome data is often complex. Perhaps ego has become too closely tied to a particular hypothesis; perhaps there are competitive pressures to be first with published results; perhaps promotion or tenure hangs on a successful research outcome; perhaps it is just the result of wishful thinking. To this potent brew we should add one further ingredient of growing importance, as science, medical research, and technology have come closer than ever to business. Universities that used to pride themselves on their arm's-length relationship to business and industry are now encouraged by cash-strapped administrators to be energetic in their search for business partners. Professors who would have previously scorned to patent their designs and techniques have no such reluctance today. Their institutions even encourage them to do so, expecting to share in the royalty receipts. Indeed, in a recent change of policy the U.S. government now permits the patenting of techniques developed with federal funds. From tobacco companies to ethical drug companies, there are lucrative contracts available for research that might produce the "right" results, and all manner of rewards open for publication of those results in authoritative journals. The temptation to cut the corners of research integrity has grown mightily as the gap between the business and research environments has narrowed.

Both in Britain and in the United States, new drugs must meet standards of safety and effectiveness in trials on human subjects before they can receive a government stamp of approval for wider use. In the past those trials were normally conducted by senior researchers in universities and medical schools whose professional reputations and scholarly credentials rested on the integrity of their research protocols. As the number of new drugs coming forward for trial increased beyond the capacity of the traditional institutions, procedures were changed. Regular doctors in practice were invited to set up sidelines to their ordinary work, testing drugs on their patients for pharmaceutical companies. The stage was set for serious research misconduct and fraud. In both countries doctors have been accused of forging the results of drug tests paid for by pharmaceutical companies. Doctors can receive handsome hourly compensation from the drug companies for recruiting patients as subjects for tests of new drugs and for reporting the results. In Britain, compensation ranges up to £200 ($320) an hour. The temptation is there for some clinicians to falsify results, forge patient signatures on consent forms, and/or recruit patients whose medical histories do not justify their inclusion in the studies. As of May 1999, the professional medical regulatory and disciplinary body in Britain (the General Medical Council) had at least ten senior doctors involved in drug testing contracts awaiting disciplinary hearings on their alleged research misconduct. In the two previous years, some thirty complaints involving research irregularities in drug testing were made to the GMC. A typical case reported in May 1999 involved a very senior professor of vascular surgery who was engaged by the Schering Health Care Company to undertake a clinical study of a blood circulation drug. The company complained to the GMC that it believed the doctor had falsified his results.[39]

Matters may not be much better in the United States. Also in May 1999, the press reported the case of Dr. Robert Fiddes: "In just a few years, Dr. Fiddes transformed his sleepy medical practice [in Whittier, California] into a research juggernaut, recruiting patients for drug experiments at a breakneck pace."[40] Dr. Fiddes was able to profit from a severe shortage in the United States of test subjects for human trials of new drugs seeking government approval: "Companies large and small showered him not only with more than 170 studies to conduct, but with millions of dollars in compensation for his work." In the late 1980s he established the Southern California Research Institute to deal with the flood of work arriving on his doorstep.

An endless series of tricks and devices was employed in the institute to help meet the enrollment targets for the studies. Patients were dragooned into studies. The results of lab tests were altered. Where necessary, bacteria were bought from suppliers and incorporated into the materials sent for testing, as if the adulterated samples had been taken from patients. X-rays were interpreted personally by Dr. Fiddes rather than by an independent radiologist so that patients who did not in fact qualify could nevertheless be included in the roster of subjects for particular drugs. If a subject's urine did not show the required abnormality for a particular test, a substitute with the appropriate disorder was called in and paid to provide the sample. Although rumors of irregularities in Dr. Fiddes's operation had been circulating for some years, it was not until 1996 that a tip led investigators to a former employee of Dr. Fiddes who could supply the details of massive research misconduct. By February 1997, federal agents raided the institute's offices and seized research and patient records, and in September 1997 Dr. Fiddes and three of his close associates pleaded guilty to conspiring to commit research fraud and to lie to investigators. His punishment has been a fifteen-month prison sentence—which may be thought to be rather lenient in light of the massive doubt he and his colleagues have cast on the safety and effectiveness of treatments that received government approval on the basis of the institute's findings.

Other temptations to unethical conduct arise from the possibility of profiting from prepublication knowledge of research results—let us call it "academic insider trading." Here is an example:

> A study published in the journal, *Annals of Internal Medicine,* showed that ingesting zinc lozenges shortened the length of a cold. One of the study's authors, Michael L. Macknin of the Cleveland Clinic Foundation, reportedly had bought stock in the company that made the lozenges before the article was published. When the company's stock soared after the journal circulated, the researcher sold some of

his shares, netting a $145,000 profit. Journal editors knew of the investment; readers did not.[41]

No one is suggesting that there had been misconduct in research or reporting in this particular study, but questions have been raised about ways to insure full disclosure of links between researchers and industry. In 1992 a study "examined 789 articles that appeared in 14 prominent scientific and medical journals. The investigators found that about one-third of the papers had at least one author with some financial interest in the research published." One response to the growing concern over potential conflicts of interest has been for journals to request authors to disclose any links they have to relevant commercial interests. The U.S. Public Health Service and the National Science Foundation have issued guidelines designed to prevent conflict of interest in grant applications.[42] The problem may have become worse since 1992. In February 2000, the *New England Journal of Medicine* admitted that nearly half (nineteen out of forty) of its printed reviews of drugs since 1997 were written by researchers with financial interest in the companies that make them, in violation of the journal's own policy. Even if the incidence of outright fraud is low, conflict of interest is not. And the mere perception that researchers and authors of scientific and medical studies have links to commercial interests tends to damage public confidence in the integrity of research and its reporting, putting at risk continued public support for research.

CONCLUSION

The public is content to call some people "professionals" not just because they have been specially trained but also because they can be trusted to act in the best interests of their clients, rather than in their own interest. When that trust is broken, society suffers damage. *Professional misconduct* is a term covering a variety of behaviors, ranging from the downright fraudulent to the merely questionable. We have noted policies forced on schools by circumstances (for example, employing unqualified teachers) and other policies leading people to act unprofessionally; we have touched on bribery "as a way of life" in some places; we have looked at ways in which students are encouraged to cheat, sometimes by their teachers' example. We have explored plagiarism and what is often the fine line between creativity and copying, as well as the intensely troubling occurrence of fraud in scientific research and reporting. However, it is worth emphasizing that the instances of misconduct we have described represent exceptions to the rule. We continue to believe that most professionals discharge their duties in a responsible and honest way. They deserve the protection that comes from vigilance in detecting misconduct by a minority of their fellows.

NOTES

1. H. Carl McCall, "Equitable and Cost-Effective School Finance Reform: Findings Resulting from the Comptroller's Community Forums on Alternatives for Financing Education," State Comptroller's Office, New York State, October 1996: table 4.
2. U.S. Department of Education, *Schools and Staffing Survey, 1993–94* (Washington, D.C.: Government Printing Office, 1995).
3. "Lowering the Raised Bar," *U.S. News and World Report*, 13 December 1999: 62–63.
4. Lynette Holloway, "Principal Is Accused of Inflating Attendance to Aid Career," *New York Times*, 17 March 2000: B3.
5. *Times Higher Education Supplement*, 19 February 1999: 15.
6. Judith O'Reilly, "Teachers Help Pupils to Cheat," *Sunday Times* (London), 31 May 1998, Internet.
7. G. A. N. Lowndes, *The Silent Social Revolution* (London: Oxford University Press, 1937), 14.
8. "Cheating Scandal Jars a Suburb of High Achievement," *New York Times*, 1 January 1992: 32.
9. "Principal Tied to a Scandal Is Retiring: Denies Tampering with Students' Tests," *New York Times*, 15 March 1997: B28.
10. Laura Williams and Dave Goldner, "Diploma Mill Eyed," *Daily News*, 25 June 1998: 4.
11. Abby Goodnough, "Teachers Said to Have Helped Students Cheat on Standard Tests," *New York Times*, 7 December 1999, Internet; Abby Goodnough, "School Cheating Inquiry Brings New Stain on Districts with Troubled Histories," *New York Times*, 13 December 1999, Internet.
12. Jodi Wilgoren, "Cheating on Statewide Tests Is Reported in Massachusetts," *New York Times*, 25 February 2000, Internet.
13. Barbara Whitaker, "Prosecutor Says Indictment of Austin Schools Will Help Deter Test Tampering," *New York Times*, 8 April 1999: 15.

14. Jon Marcus, "Curtain on US 'Sports Students' Farce Rises," *Times Higher Education Supplement*, 3 September 1999: 10.

15. Judith O'Reilly, "Heads Accused of Rigging School Inspections," *Times* (London), 8 March 1998, Internet.

16. "Campaign for Driving-Test Style Checks," *Times Educational Supplement*, 20 October 1995, Internet.

17. Lucy Ward, "Auditors Call for Fraud Clampdown," *Times Educational Supplement*, 14 June 1996: 23.

18. Maurice Chittenden, "Fraud Investigators Probe Private College Firm," *Sunday Times* (London), 14 February 1999, Internet.

19. See http://www.heartland.org/education/november/kentucky.htm, Internet. See also Steve Stecklow, "Apple Polishing: Kentucky's Teachers Get Bonuses, but Some Are Caught Cheating—if Their Schools Score Well, State Ponies Up Cash; Lots of Grade Inflation—Bus Drivers Seek Their Share," *Wall Street Journal*, 2 September 1997: A1.

20. John J. Cannell, *Nationally Normed Educational Achievement Testing in America's Public Schools: How All Fifty States Are Above the National Average* (Daniels, W.V.: Friends for Education, 1987); John J. Cannell, *How Public Educators Cheat on Standardized Achievement Tests: The "Lake Wobegone" Report* (Albuquerque, N.M.: Friends for Education, 1989).

21. Yojarna Sharma, "No Thanks for the Memories," *Times Educational Supplement*, 13 September 1996, Internet.

22. Paul Telfer, "Who's Cheating Now?" *Times Educational Supplement*, 20 July 1990: 19.

23. Adam Sherwin, "Children Account for Mobile Sales Surge," *Times* (London), 6 January 2000, Internet.

24. Francis Rafferty, "The Future Is Cheating—at £16 per Hour," *Times Educational Supplement*, 5 December 1997, Internet.

25. "Cheating Rife in the Universities," *Independent on Sunday*, 12 September 1999, Internet.

26. Ralph Blumental with Sarah Lyall, "Plagiarism Accusations Halt Distribution of John Paul Jones Biography," *New York Times*, 21 September 1999, Internet.

27. *Harper and Row v. Brian Sutton-Smith and Prentice-Hall*, No. 73 Civ. 5446 United States District Court for the Southern District of New York, 413 F. Supp. 385, 1975.

28. Alan Dundes, "Bruno Bettelheim's Uses of Enchantment and Abuses of Scholarship," *Journal of American Folklore* 104 (winter 1991): 74–83.

29. Richard Pollak, *The Creation of Dr. B: A Biography of Bruno Bettelheim* (New York: Simon and Schuster, 1996).

30. Jürgen Renn and Robert Schulmann, eds., *Albert Einstein, Mileva Maric: The Love Letters*, Shawn Smith, trans. (Princeton, N.J.: Princeton University Press, 1992).

31. Robert K. Merton, *The Sociology of Science: Theoretical and Empirical Investigations* (Chicago: University of Chicago Press, 1973).

32. John F. Kelly and Phillip K. Wearne, *Tainting Evidence: Inside the Scandals at the FBI Crime Lab* (New York: Free Press, 1998).

33. Committee on Publication Ethics, *The COPE Report, 1998* (London: British Medical Journal, 1998), Internet.

34. S. Lock and F. Wells, eds., *Fraud and Misconduct in Medical Research* (London: BMJ Publishing Group, 1996); Daniel J. Kevles, *The Baltimore Case: A Trial of Politics, Science, and Character* (New York: W.W. Norton, 1998); Robert Bell, *Impure Science: Fraud, Compromise and Political Influence in Scientific Research* (New York: Wiley, 1992); David J. Miller and Michael Hersen, eds., *Research Fraud in the Behavioral and Biomedical Sciences* (New York: Wiley, 1992); *Scientific Fraud: Hearings before the Subcommittee on Oversight and Investigations of the Committee on Energy and Commerce, House of Representatives, One Hundred Second Congress, First Session, on Apparent Wrongdoing at the NIH Laboratory of Tumor Cell Biology and Actions Involving the Office of Scientific Integrity* (6 March and 1 August 1991).

35. L. J. Kamin, *The Science and Politics of I.Q.* (Potomac, M.D.: Lawrence Erlbaum, 1974); L. J. Kamin, "Burt's I.Q. Data," *Science* 195 (1977): 246–48; L. S. Hearnshaw, *Cyril Burt, Psychologist* (Ithaca, N.Y.: Cornell University Press, 1979); Robert B. Joynson, "Fallible Judgements," *Society* 31 (March–April 1994): 45ff; N. J. MacKintosh, ed., *Cyril Burt: Fraud or Framed?* (London: Oxford University Press, 1995).

36. "Misconduct in Research: Editors Respond," *British Medical Journal* 315 (26 July 1997), 201.

37. "Treatment and Prevention: What Is COPE and Why?" *The COPE Report*, 1998, Internet.

38. Khadija Magardie, "Disgraced Bezwoda Misled His Patients," *Mail and Guardian*, 2 February 2000: 10; Denise Grady, "Breast Cancer Researcher Admits Falsifying Data," *New York Times*, 5 February 2000, Internet.

39. Lois Rogers, "Top Doctor Accused of Fiddling Drug Tests," *Sunday Times* (London), 30 May 1999, Internet.

40. Kurt Eichenwald and Gina Kolata, "A Doctor's Drug Trials Turn into Fraud: Research for Hire," *New York Times*, 17 May 1999: A1, A16–A17.

41. Gary Stix, "The Ties that Bind," *Scientific American*, March 1999, Internet.

42. Stix, "The Ties that Bind."

Chapter 5

Integrity: Countering Fraud

Integrity: The character of uncorrupted virtue. Uprightness, honesty, sincerity. Soundness of moral principle.

FRAUD AND ITS CORRELATES

At the very beginning of this work we suggest that cheating in exams is as old as exams themselves, that cheating occurs in every country where exams are organized, and that wherever credentials are valued, there also credentials fraud will be found. Obtaining good results in exams has always been important, but it is of paramount importance when exam results open or close avenues to higher steps on the education ladder, to the most remunerative career paths, and to upper social status. The greater the value of good exam results, the more the incentives for misconduct increase.

Our survey of cheating in exams around the world describes the many techniques and devices employed and also takes note of the growing technological sophistication that modern electronic means of communication have introduced. These extend from illicit copying and theft of exam questions, to impersonation of test takers, and even to teachers tampering with answer sheets and scores. Neither rules and regulations nor severe penalties have prevented the continuance and even increase of cheating. Popular alternatives to traditional exams, such as assigned coursework and profiles of performance, have in fact opened additional avenues.

Despite the problems raised by cheating, exams continue to guard critical transition points in educational progress and to determine entry to advanced education, professions, and public service. The marks of success are often revealed in credentials. Porter has even suggested that, since the U.S. Constitution forbade conferring titles of rank, Americans have come to use degrees and other credentials as substitutes.[1]

In chapter 3 we describe the flourishing industry of the diploma mill, currently defined by the U.S. Department of Education as "an organization that awards degrees without requiring its students to meet educational standards for such degrees—it either receives fees from its so-called students on the basis of fraudulent misrepresentation, or it makes it possible for the recipients of its degrees to perpetrate fraud on the public." As we review the extent of diploma mills and the availability of their services, it is evident that their appealing wares are within everyone's easy reach. Printed advertising and publicity material, and now the facilities afforded by the Internet, make degrees from impressive-sounding, but fake, colleges easily and quickly available in return for little effort. Relatively low cost adds to the attraction—a few hundred dollars for a bachelor's degree and a couple of thousand for a Ph.D.—with a genuine-looking diploma and transcript thrown in. The advertisements make the pitch more plausible by referring to "state authorization" (a meaningless boast, at least as far as academic quality is concerned) or being "accredited" (almost invariably also from captive organizations).

Because no central ministry of education exists in the United States, there is in effect no official national organization to regulate these activities. At best, national professional groups may exert influence. The federal authorities do have power to prosecute diploma mills, but only when mail fraud, deceptive advertising, or other fraudulent commercial practices are involved. Although most states in the United States have established control systems, there is no uniform national code of requirements. Instead, each state determines how and to what extent it will assume regulatory powers. Some states (Hawaii, for example) leave it to their regular consumer protection agencies; other states have handed regulatory authority to their boards of education (Ohio). Some states are woefully lax in their pursuit of fraudulent degree-awarding outfits; others pursue them with vigor, driving them away to operate in less hostile environments.

For some infractions—those that are clearly illegal—the specifics must be spelled out in state laws identifying which actions are wrong and what the consequences are. In New York, for example, impersonation of a candidate for a state exam is a misdemeanor punishable by a fine and/or imprisonment up to one year; in other states, institutions and individuals are culpable if they claim to offer study programs and credentials that are false. In some cases they can be sued for dishonesty in advertising by the relevant state authority, usually the department of consumer affairs. But a department of state concerned with accreditation of institutions and their awards is probably the more common and best way of keeping this aspect of the process clean. In those states where these bodies do not exist, or where they neglect their watchdog functions, diploma mills spring up overnight and appear well able to keep ahead of regulation and the law. The result of the patchwork of state regulation and the absence of a coherent federal presence has been to permit a most unfortunate and damaging proliferation of opportunities for credentials fraud.

This has by no means been costless. When individuals engage in academic fraud they are as likely to be cheating themselves, as much as they are cheating the educational and credentialing systems. Students who cheat or plagiarize are foregoing learning opportunities otherwise open to them, as are those who purchase or steal faked credentials. Extensive cheating imposes large costs on society, in terms of loss of confidence in the integrity and fairness of the education and exam systems. In like manner, quickie and intrinsically worthless degrees stain the reputation of the educational system as a whole. Legitimate institutions offering "distance education" and "credit for life experience" are brought into disrepute. Particularly damaging is the effect of these dubious institutions and their phony degrees on foreign perceptions of U.S. degrees in general.

In chapter 4 we focus on professional misconduct in education and research. We suggest that a number of educational policies in the United States actually promote fraud, if only unintentionally. For example, inequalities in district funding combined with a high degree of local control lead to sharp differences in the quality of schooling in neighboring communities. Parents are thereby tempted to provide fictional addresses for their children, so that they can attend better schools in other districts.

Another policy that motivates misconduct is the common use of students' standardized test scores to reward or penalize schools. Teachers and administrators are tempted to help students cheat or to tamper with the answer sheets before submitting them for grading.

School systems cheat students via the common practice of social promotion. Promoting pupils to the next grade according to their age rather than their academic achievement results in graduation without minimum knowledge and skills. More fraud occurs when a school district lowers the passing level because too many students have failed, just as when it employs unqualified teachers to teach them.

Plagiarism and the fabrication of results are the twin bugbears of research in all fields. Plagiarism is an extension of exam cheating by copying. Pressure to obtain financial support from outside sources and to produce "grant-worthy" results tempts individuals and institutions to falsify their work, even to the extent of fabricating data. When private industry sponsors university research, the desire to show quick and useful results favoring the sponsor's products may be well-nigh irresistible.

What are some of the correlates of cheating, corruption, and other forms of fraud in education and research? Bribery and corruption in business affairs may be regarded as indicators of the degree of general misconduct in a society. The reports of an anticorruption pressure group, Transparency International (see chapter 1), indicate that some societies, primarily the poorer countries of the world, are perceived as being saturated with business fraud; others, typically the wealthier, First World countries, much less so. The incidence of cheating and other forms of fraud in education appears to follow a similar pattern.

Greaney and Kellaghan, in their international study of exams, note that there is more opportunity for corruption in developing countries. The absence of a trained and trustworthy bureaucracy, the limited paths out of poverty, and the dominance of such cultural values as loyalty to one's own family, tribe, or clan (rather than to some distant, impersonal, official organization) are conditions conducive to cheating and corruption, at least by the standards of the Western nations.

GRAY AREAS

Questionable conduct takes place in a social and cultural context that shapes views of what is acceptable. Fraud and various forms of cheating may even be held to be virtues when they express family or group solidarity. When, if ever, is fraud not a fraud? When, if ever, is it not dishonest to cheat? When, if ever, is the buying and selling of credentials defensible?

Diploma Mills

Consider some of the justifications given by diploma mill owners in defense of their practices. They claim simply to provide a service wanted by the public—and to do so at an affordable price. How basically different, they ask, are their actions from those of fully accredited "reputable" colleges that graduate students who have remained essentially uneducated or, for that matter, of grade schools that graduate students who can barely read and write? In what way is their business essentially different from that of institutions that do not hesitate before awarding honorary degrees to affluent donors?

A further justification argues that what is called cheating, the purchase of credentials and other forms of fraud, is simply a way of dealing with a system that is fundamentally unjust and, in fact, corrupt. The inequities built into the system justify undermining it. The past and present sins of political oppression, especially in the formerly colonized areas of the world, provide the most common rationale for these assertions. Most of the colonized indigenous peoples regarded the colonizer's state as an alien institution and felt justified in withholding their allegiance.[2] This attitude persisted after independence: Cheating the state, or its institutions, was a legitimate activity, not one to be deplored. Easy access to credentials, it is also claimed, "levels the playing field" for those individuals whose progress has been impeded by misfortune earlier in life by poor previous educational opportunities, disadvantageous social or economic conditions, or racial prejudice.

Plagiarism

Ambiguity about what constitutes acceptable behavior frequently occurs when plagiarism is charged. Even honest students often do not understand what constitutes plagiarism in practice, and they will express surprise upon being accused of it. They have been taught to depend on authorities and sources and to use the information and ideas of others. Are the errors they make merely technicalities in which the proper form of footnoting and acknowledgment is lacking? Is plagiarism averted by simple paraphrase of the original? For many students these are not easy questions to answer.

The general availability and extensive use of the Internet complicates the situation even more. In an article titled "Peek Performance: Does the Internet Create More Cheaters, or More Skillful Ones?" the *Boston Globe* reports on a problem at Dartmouth College. Students in an introductory computer course were shown by their instructor how to do an Internet assignment. The professor apparently did not secure the website containing the answers, and students who took advantage of his oversight were charged with cheating. Dartmouth administrators absolved them, even though some were believed to have obtained their answers from the website. Is this analogous to copying material "off the blackboard" or from a library source, to use pre-electronic terms? Were they merely omitting the source? Difficult as it is to determine who had actually copied material, there is no doubt that the Internet makes more information available and much easier to obtain.[3]

Parental Help

A fourth grade student is given an assignment by his teacher. He is required in two weeks time to present in class a description of the difference between the daily diets of Americans and Chinese. His mother, who typically helps with her son's homework, goes to the local library, selects some books on everyday life in China, identifies relevant passages, photocopies them in the library, and gives them to her son, having highlighted the most important sentences. Is all of that acceptable? Opinions might well differ.

Some might say, "Yes, it's unconditionally acceptable because it's good for parents to involve themselves in this way in their child's homework." Others might say, "No, it's unconditionally improper because it's a kind of cheating and anyway denies the son the opportunity to browse in the library and to learn by doing the skills of library-based inquiry." Yet others may judge it to be conditionally OK, as long as the young student declares somewhere in his presentation the extent of help received: "I wish to acknowledge the help I have received from my mother, who . . . "!!

At some point, it is argued, parental help must be judged excessive. For example, identifying major themes for the student to consider lies at the far edge of acceptability, but writing out some of the text for the student to copy falls into impropriety. But even such a verdict cannot always settle the question. Perhaps there is no universal rule. Perhaps what is acceptable with regard to one student is not acceptable with regard to another. A sick, home-bound child might justifiably be given more help than an ordinary student. But what about one who is heavily engaged in school athletics, in the school play or the band, or has accepted an unusually heavy academic load? Do the student's time-pressures justify more parental help with homework than "normal"? If each case must be judged on its situational merits, the gray areas grow ever larger.

Parents Manipulating Test Conditions

Currently, just under 2 percent of all SAT candidates are given special dispensation to take more than the standard three hours on the tests. Almost one-quarter of all candidates do not complete the full test before time is up, so extra time can be a significant advantage. Extra time is afforded to those who apply on such grounds as suffering from reading disability, dyslexia, physical impairment, and the like. However, there is good evidence that alongside the genuine applications, there are many that are unjustified. A far-reaching investigation of possible abuse was reported in the *Los Angeles Times*.[4] The report is based on an analysis of data supplied by the College Board, which owns the SAT. It shows that a disproportionate number of white, male candidates from homes in wealthy districts and/or attending private schools in the Northeast or in advantaged areas in California were enjoying extra time. For example, at twenty private schools in the Northeast, the percentage of SAT candidates in the extra time category was five times higher than the national average of 1.9 percent. In California, the report states, not one SAT candidate out of the 1,439 entered from ten inner-city Los Angeles–region schools got a special time allowance. Meanwhile, the percentages of candidates from selected private and public high schools in wealthier areas receiving extra time were also way above the national average. One commentator is quoted as remarking, "Something is out of whack." Of course, what is out of whack is the use of doubtful medical certificates by better educated, wealthier, and better connected parents to obtain special and undeserved privilege for their children.

Teachers' Special Knowledge

Teachers accumulate knowledge of the kinds of questions that appear on tests and exams and even of the structure and content of those questions. Sometimes this knowledge comes from years of experience and observation. Sometimes it comes from some degree of "privileged" access: Perhaps they or their close professional associates are involved in setting the questions. Moreover, the publications of the testing organizations describe the basic configurations of the tests and give examples of questions.

Students benefit from instruction in test taking, advice on what questions are likely to come up, and suggestions for how to answer them. However, unlike in most countries of the world, "teaching to the test" is generally frowned on in the United States, although U.S. students will often ask their teachers, "Is this going to be on the test?" When teachers "teach to the test," are they doing something perfectly acceptable, clearly professional, and in the best interests of their students? Or are they narrowing the scope of their instruction so severely that their students are shortchanged in terms of their education, however much they might profit in terms of their eventual test scores? Does judgment turn on how the teacher came by his or her special knowledge? Or is "teaching to the test" laudatory if the test is a "good" one and not so praiseworthy if the test is narrow and poorly constructed?

Should teachers prepare summaries of material for their students to study before the exam, which is a common practice? If that is acceptable, what about sample answers written out in extenso? Students have been penalized for presenting in their exams model answers that they were trained to write.[5] How does training in answering specific exam questions relate to "good instruction"? Where does an unacceptable degree of spoonfeeding begin?—a moot question for educators to consider. Any judgment must attend to the particulars of both student and context.

Teachers' Qualifications

It is estimated that about one-third of U.S secondary public school teachers are teaching subjects they did not study during their higher education and training. Does this amount to fraud practiced by school board employers on students, parents, and eventual employers? Is it better to have at least somebody teaching in the classroom, however ill-prepared from the standpoint of formal qualifications, than to have nobody at all? Having nobody at all will probably mean larger class sizes. Which is better?

Different school boards make different determinations, based most probably on the funds they have available to attract and retain the fully qualified teachers they ideally should have. Perhaps the fault lies not so much with the school district and its administrators as at the state level, where excessively large financial inequalities among the state's school districts continue to be tolerated. We have found no record of school principals or districts announcing that they will not appoint unqualified teachers to teach subjects/classes and that as a consequence those subjects/classes will remain "uncovered" (except possibly in optional subjects, often relegated to lesser importance, such as music and art).

Massaging Credentials

There is nothing gray about the outright falsification of credentials, such as awarding oneself a completely fictitious degree from a university one never attended. This is not uncommon, and it is just plain wrong. But what about a situation in which a student's college or university career dragged on somewhat longer than usual? Perhaps the student dropped out for a year or two for academic, emotional, or financial reasons. Is he or she absolutely required to state the facts baldly in a resume? Or can a resume slide delicately over the matter, perhaps by omission rather than overt falsification of dates? Where exactly is the line to be drawn?

Another student didn't quite finish his doctoral degree. Yes, he completed all his coursework and even made a good start on his dissertation but somehow never managed to present and defend it. Perhaps his dissertation committee dissolved through retirements, relocations, or professorial conflict of ideas—anyway, through no fault of the candidate. His resume carefully describes his academic progression: this college for his bachelor's, that university for his master's, and yet a further university for his doctoral study, the latter particularly carefully documented. Of course, nowhere does it baldly and falsely announce "Ph.D., awarded 19—," but it does give the title of the (never presented, undefended) dissertation and even a brief abstract of its contents. The total effect implies that an ABD ("all but dissertation") involved quite as much effort and achievement as a completed doctoral degree. No lies are told, but the whole truth is not revealed. Is this marginally acceptable? deceitful, with extenuating circumstances? or wrong, wrong, wrong?

University Ethics

Universities make a business of garnering donations to build their endowments, extend their real estate, and establish academic chairs. They prefer unrestricted gifts, but most large gifts are restricted. They come with strings attached, conditions specifying the purposes for which the capital and/or income may and may not be used. Sometimes the proposed strings are so restrictive that the university simply refuses the gift; sometimes the strings are there, but they have been set out somewhat loosely in the deed of gift. The intention of the donor is clear, and the university has agreed to accept the gift on the terms stated but in the knowledge that loopholes exist and might come in handy at a future date.

For example, at one time Harvard University accepted the gift of a tract of virgin forest in New York State (the Stillman Bequest), to be kept as an unspoiled, unmanaged forest, forever wild, and to be used in field training of Harvard forestry students. Over time, a forestry program became a burden for Harvard, and by 1975 the university proposed to sell the forest and place the proceeds in its general endowment. The donor was by this time dead, but his family protested what they considered to be a violation of the donor's intention and especially the spirit, if not the letter, of the deed of gift. Harvard eventually secured a court judgment, permitting the university to do as it wished with the forest.[6] The law is on the university's side, but where does the university's moral obligation lie? Harvard pleads that it can make better educational use of the disputed property than maintaining a forest for the use of a few students. Should it have the right to overrule the stated intentions of the donor, intentions that it freely agreed to honor? Opinion will most likely differ, governed by the dictum: "Tell me where you sit, and I'll tell you where you stand."

Consider another common situation. A university receives a large donation for a building, a new academic chair, or a new institute. What is an ethically acceptable acknowledgment by the university of the donor's generosity? How far can the university go? Is it OK to look favorably on the admission application of the donor's son/daughter/niece/nephew/friend? How about the university press accepting the book manuscript of the donor's spouse for publication? Or is the ethical limit an honorary degree at the next commencement ceremony? or just the donor's name on the building or attached to the chair or institute?

Federal grant money is a significant source of university income for research and/or the provision of specified services. The university is allowed to add onto its direct costs of wages, salaries, employee benefits, equipment, and the like an amount to cover its pro rata costs of accommodating and administering the project. These are the so-called indirect costs or "overhead" on the contract, the prime area where universities typically engage in creative accounting. Indirect costs are based on the total costs of administering the university and the proportion of each category of the total that can be justifiably ascribed to the project. So it becomes advantageous to push up the accounting costs of administration as high as possible. Stanford got into trouble with the federal government for (among other things) including in its reckoning of total university administrative costs the cost of providing the president's house with a regular supply of fresh flowers. The government did not think this was acceptable, and Stanford had to repay overhead funds it had already received. Certainly from a regulatory perspective Stanford was in the wrong; the ethical question may not be so clear. Universities have consistently claimed that the federal government does not reimburse them fully for the true costs of the grants and contracts they operate. They do not see much wrong with shoehorning into their total administrative costs all they can get away with by padding their allocation to the administration of the grants.

Some debate has recently taken place on the activities of "Campus Pipeline," which is signing up campuses around the country for free websites, contingent on permitting commercial advertising. These websites, which will provide a variety of services (including course lists, information on accommodations and forthcoming events, and campus news) are seen as highly useful but too expensive for a college to create on its own. Some see this as a further incursion of commercial values into the world of education, on a par with Mr. Whittle's Channel One. Others, however, point to ads carried by student newspapers and the operations of the college bookstore and ask, "How is a commercially sponsored website different?"

A similar development has popped up in the form of scholarship lotteries on the Internet. "Free" scholarships are offered to surfers who are prepared to supply some information about themselves. The sites are financed by advertisers and marketers who hope to attract business. One such site is at www.freescholarships.com. It offers one daily prize of $10,000, one monthly prize of $25,000, and a quarterly prize of $25,000. It claims Microsoft as one of its "partners" and offers links to information about colleges, study aids, other sources of financial aid, and the like. The site opened for business in early February 2000 and was promptly so overwhelmed with would-be registrants that its computers crashed under the strain. As of the time of writing, the site appears to have overcome its initial problems, publishes a regular list of daily winners, and gives every appearance of legitimacy. Obviously, a registrant's chances of winning are slim, and a player must visit the site each day to be entered in the next day's draw. So, does this enterprise represent an unwarranted and unwelcome intrusion of commercial and even gambling values into education, or is it a resourceful device to help at least a few lucky winners ease their financial problems? Opinions will no doubt differ.

Publication of Research

"Publish or perish" is a virtual law of survival for research personnel, whether in universities or in specialized research institutions. The pressure to get published (and in scientific fields to get published first) is intense. An applicant's record of publication is a major factor considered by appointment and promotion committees, as well as by funding agencies. The result is some unknown (and perhaps unknowable) degree of misconduct in research and publication practices, some of which is clearly wrong but some of which may be dubious, though not necessarily unacceptable.

If the number of published papers is an important criterion for professional advancement, then it is clearly wrong for an author to submit virtually the same paper to different journals, perhaps with only a slight change in title or opening words. But what about carefully staging the submission of manuscripts so that it takes four or five papers to cover the entire research "story," rather than submitting just one large one? That will certainly look more impressive on the researcher's resume and might be justified as simply playing the game according to the letter of the rules.

Senior professors, who have a number of juniors working in their research labs, should presumably not list their names first on papers reporting work done entirely by those juniors. But should they put their names on the papers at all? This is common practice justified perhaps by the fact that the labs are after all the senior professors', and the juniors worked in their labs on problems presumably OK'd by senior professors. Even more important, by listing his or her name the senior professor acknowledges a degree of responsibility for the accuracy of the research and the reporting. But there are gray areas and marginal cases to worry about. Some juniors may very well feel that their contributions are not being recognized as fully as they should be, that the senior professor is grabbing the headlines and the kudos of a major, newsworthy development. Once again, it's a question of "Tell me where you sit, and I'll tell you where you stand."

School System Policies

When too many aspiring educators failed Massachusetts's first basic reading and writing test for teachers, the Board of Education proposed to lower the passing grade in order to reduce the number of failures, thereby demonstrating that standards and test cutoff points are largely arbitrary.[7] Despite the outrage expressed in some quarters, such practices are not at all rare, and educational quality inevitably suffers.

Another common school district practice is to exclude or discourage some poor achievers and non-English-speaking students from taking external exams. Such students may be encouraged to stay home that day or may be given an alternative assignment. While there may be nothing wrong with teachers shielding students from a test that is too difficult for them, keeping poor students from participating in an assessment so that the class or school average will not be dragged down is highly questionable.

A recent and continuing issue in schools is grade inflation. Despite declines in scores on the SAT exam, for the past twenty years average grades in school and in postsecondary education have been moving up. Private schools in New York City have virtually abolished the F grade, considering it, according to one source, "insufficiently nurturing." Brearley School, for example, records "weak" rather than "F," while Brooklyn Friends School uses "needs additional growth." An article in *Link,* a college magazine (April–May 1995), drew attention to this trend and its implication in a story headlined "How Grade Inflation Is Degrading Your Degree." The author cites studies that show how the lowest grades are becoming rarer, at least in the humanities and social sciences, so that a grade of A is no longer an unequivocal indicator of excellence. Grades function as "academic currency." In previous times, the practice of clipping and debasing gold and silver coinage drew deserved condemnation as a fraud on the public. Today, when superior academic grades are casually awarded by so many instructors, a similar fraud is being perpetrated on students, parents, and others who would like to rely on transcripts as a guide to their decision making.[8]

Clearly fraudulent or not, misconduct in education and research can never be welcome. It follows that a major societal task is to reduce as much as possible both the incidence and the severity of fraud.

COUNTERING DISHONESTY AND FRAUD

We can identify four major approaches to the task of countering academic misconduct:

- reducing incentives for fraud;
- reducing opportunities for fraud and maximizing the probability of detection;
- defining and publicizing the limits of acceptable conduct and clarifying, advertising, and enforcing sanctions;
- building an academic community that regards cheating, plagiarism, and the like as simply unthinkable.

Reducing Incentives

The major incentive to cheat in school, college, university, and the professions, to plagiarize, fabricate research, and offer false credentials, derives from the intense competitive pressures that have built up everywhere in contemporary societies and their institutions. We need to understand that there is an important downside to the emphasis on testing in the public schools: The more testing, the more incentive there is to cheat—not only for students but also for teachers, principals, and other administrative staff. Similarly, the more emphasis on credentials as the passport to jobs, the greater the incentive to embellishment and falsification. Students are intensely conscious of their grade point averages, class rankings, SAT scores, and the standing of the colleges that accept (and reject) them. Not only is school and college sport suffused with the spirit of competition, but the entire system of tests and exams is designed to rank individuals in some order of perceived merit, usually for the purpose of allocating limited opportunities for further study or employment.

Universities compete vigorously for federal government research contracts, and among researchers themselves the quest for grant money is a major preoccupation. Publications such as *U.S. News & World Report* print annual rankings of the "quality" of colleges and universities. Everywhere one looks in the academic and research scenes, competition is a fact of life—not perhaps as intense as it is in the worlds of business and finance but nonetheless palpable. In such an environment, inducements to cheat and cut corners are strong, for not only are the potential rewards of doing well great, the penalties for failure are severe. Any successful program to reduce misconduct needs to tackle the prevalence and intensity of competition—no easy task in a society suffused with the spirit of competition.

None of this should be taken as an argument for abandoning competition in all its forms. First, that simply cannot be done, and, second, some amount of competition in the world of education and research is a valuable spur to effort. But we should be careful not to overdo the promotion of a winners-and-losers mentality, to the extent that the "bads" of competition outweigh the "goods." That is what has happened in the world of professional sport, where every day brings its new scandal of drug-taking, money-chasing, and unsporting behavior—all in response to the intense competitive pressures felt by players, teams, managers, and coaches.

Reducing Opportunities

While there is no justification at all for assuming that all exam takers and applicants for positions lie and cheat, a lively suspicion that, given the opportunity, some people will cut corners is reasonable. People in responsible positions need to learn about the kinds of fraud and deception that typically occur in their areas of responsibility, and they should seek to arrange matters so that the opportunities available for misconduct are minimized.

The entire process of constructing, printing, and distributing test materials must be guarded against abuses by the personnel involved. Administration of tests must be secure and be known to be secure. Proctors at exams must reduce the opportunities for cheating and be on the lookout for it. In high-stakes exams, if candidates' identities are not carefully checked, the way is open for impersonation. If the provision of appropriate seating arrangements is neglected, cheating is facilitated. When proctors are lax in enforcing obvious precautions, perhaps permitting students to leave the room without proper supervision, to converse and signal to each other, even surreptitiously to consult materials they have brought in with them, they have failed in their clear duty to minimize opportunities for misconduct. In so doing, they are guilty of acting against the interest of honest candidates and of betraying an important trust. For this reason alone, administrators should take care to assign only properly trained and responsible persons to the task of test proctoring.

In similar vein, opportunities to pass off fraudulent credentials should be minimized. Organizations need to work at creating an expectation that fraud will probably be detected. In this way, applicants' tendencies to indulge in creative writing on their resumes will be deterred. Staff members responsible for interviews, appointments, and promotions need to be trained and alert to the possibilities of embellishment, false documents, and the like. Too often, checking of credentials is neglected or left to the judgment of unqualified personnel, with unfortunate results.

Editors of scientific journals have to be particularly careful that they are not made unwitting accomplices to the publication of fraudulent research reports. The tradition has been to rely on peer reviews of manuscripts to catch fraud and plagiarism. Editors are becoming aware that they need to supplement peer review with other procedures: calling for submission of supporting documentation, requesting facilities for onsite inspection, insisting on delays in publication while other researchers try to duplicate results, requiring assurances that the research data have been properly archived and can be made available on request. These and similar precautions are useful for reducing opportunities for fraudulent publication. COPE (the association of editors of medical journals in Britain) has been so doubtful about its ability to counter all of the fraud it suspects occurs that it has called for the establishment of "an independent body to counter fraud, plagiarism and other misconduct committed by doctors and scientists in their eagerness for academic status."[9]

Clarifying, Advertising, and Enforcing Sanctions

While college instructors often assume that first-year students know the proper conventions regarding the use of published authors' work, the fact is that many do not. Beginners may need to be instructed in the rules in order to avoid charges of plagiarism. Otherwise, only too often they will copy material (with or without acknowledgment) and present it as their own. Schools and colleges would also do well to define carefully for students when collaboration on academic tasks is acceptable and when it is not. Doing so will help diminish unpleasant accusations by faculty and resentment on the part of students.

Similarly, the penalties for infringing the rules need to be carefully spelled out and mechanisms for their enforcement set up and used, with appropriate announcement. The aim is to have all members of the academic community made aware that the institution takes these matters seriously and has prepared itself to deal with infractions.

As we have pointed out, in the United States at present credentials fraud is ineffectively tackled. The United States would certainly profit from having a national advisory council on academic fraud to serve as a clearinghouse for information on scams, major incidents of misconduct, and suspect institutions. If such a board could also assist states in strengthening their legislation and administrative control of diploma mills, that would be even more helpful. Best of all would be a Uniform Code of Academic Conduct, available for state authorities to adopt or adapt.

Most recommendations for fighting fraud in education and research are cast in terms of the following: reducing the incentives to break the rules, as well as the opportunities for doing so; clarifying and publicizing the rules of the institution or profession; and perhaps increasing the likelihood that infractions will be detected and punished. It is common ground that although misconduct cannot be entirely eliminated, fraud needs to be pursued energetically if confidence in the system is to be maintained. Because most people are unaware of the extent of fraud and falsification, and because most people in academe take the view that control and punishment are someone else's business (even when it occurs under their own noses), more effort than ever is needed to counter misconduct.

Some skepticism is in order here. After all, there is already a good deal of rule making and proctoring, and given the increasing volume and incidence of fraud, it cannot be claimed that the rule-making, legalistic, punitive approach has been a great success. A cautionary parallel is the so-called War on Drugs, which may have clogged the courts and filled the prisons but arguably has not diminished the amount of drug use and abuse in America.

Making Fraud Unacceptable

An alternative approach to controlling fraud in education emphasizes the need to create academic communities in which fraud is just not acceptable, either to students or to instructors and administrators. In this vein, schools, colleges, and universities are urged to be completely open about their abhorrence of cheating on exams and course assignments, as well as of plagiarism and other manifestations of inappropriate copying. They are urged to draw their entire academic community—students, faculty, and administrators—into the business of formulating and announcing a reasoned, negative community-wide stance toward academic misconduct. The aim should be to build an institutional culture in which cheating and plagiarism are condemned as something that "our people" just don't do. In this way, it is argued, rules and regulations, enforcement and penalties, become minor aspects of the academic scene. All members of the campus community will have integrated in their own attitudes and behavior a set of expectations and values that makes the regulatory and punitive approach not only unnecessary but even counterproductive.

This approach, too, has its difficulties. Values and attitudes in academe reflect values and attitudes in the wider society, which is far from being suffused with communitarian ideas and ideals. To expect individuals in academe to be able to overcome the pressures all around them to compete is something of a long shot. Honor codes have been adopted by some institutions in the hope that they will help reduce student cheating. The codes can be thought of as a kind of halfway house between the punitive and the communitarian approaches to the control of academic misconduct. There is evidence that honor codes do help reduce the incidence of cheating. However, they are designed to affect the behavior of students, while (as we hope this book has amply demonstrated) the problems of academic misconduct extend far beyond the currently enrolled student body.

In chapter 2 we note several approaches to contain cheating in tests and exams: mainly easily adopted, commonsense measures to alert teachers, administrators, and proctors. In chapter 3 we point to two factors that make credentials fraud more difficult to control: its global scope and the power of the modern technology of document reproduction and communications. Also in chapters 3 and 4 we have noted the efforts of governmental authorities and professional organizations to publicize and restrain the abuse of credentials and professional misconduct. The record we have assembled shows the continuing need for vigilance (and action) to counter fraud in its many manifestations.

Finally, we need to recognize that the business of trying to control academic misconduct faces exactly the same kind of dilemma confronting attempts to control other kinds of criminal or antisocial behavior. The greater the reliance on regulatory, legalistic, and punitive mechanisms, the less chance there is that programs based on fostering a community ethos against such behavior will take root. At the same time, too much reliance on the building of community culture runs the risk that inveterate cheaters will take advantage of weak sanctions and lax enforcement. Once that happens and gets known, others previously less inclined to misconduct will say to themselves, "Well, if they're doing it, getting away with it, and profiting from it, why not me, too?"

CONCLUSION

Five years after shaming their school by cheating to win a statewide academic contest, some of the former Steinmetz High School students on the quiz team now say they have a single regret: being caught.[10]

The newspaper article in which this amazingly candid report appears describes a school team's conspiracy to cheat in an academic decathlon. The conspiracy began with a student stealing a copy of the test paper. The team's teacher-coach then helped the team to prepare their answers and urged them to maintain secrecy about their misconduct. In the event, their grades on the test were just too good. An investigation revealed the cheating, and the team's results were cancelled. But five years later the students and their teacher expressed no remorse. Instead, they offered an assortment of justifications for their despicable behavior. Paraphrasing, they run as follows: "We were up against a high-powered academically and socially superior school, so we did what was necessary to win"; "The other school had advantages that we did not have. We were simply leveling the playing field"; "We felt we were being bullied and condescended to by the superior attitudes of the other team, so we took them down a peg or two"; and finally, "You tell us who has the right to point an accusing finger at us, when everybody around is cheating. Hey, the president of the school board had just been jailed for tax evasion." Not the faintest suspicion of moral understanding is conveyed in these self-serving justifications. They reveal a frightening readiness to resort to unfair means to attain a desired end.

In the end, the quality of a society depends on how it educates its young people and how it selects and prepares them to fulfill their various roles as citizens, as experts, as professionals. No social effort is more important. John Locke, a seventeenth-century English philosopher, recognized this central point over 300 years ago when he wrote, "Virtue is harder to be got than knowledge of the world; and, if lost in a young man, is seldom recovered."[11]

Misconduct in education and research directly threatens the quality of a society, now and for the future. It erodes confidence in the integrity of important institutions, devalues credentials, and reduces the effectiveness of the workforce. In education, it calls into question the whole process of selection, training, and certification of future citizens. In research, it undercuts a powerful system of discovering new knowledge and testing its truth.

We conclude with the recognition that we are touching on an age-old philosophical issue: how to instill virtue into people and their institutions and how to create a more moral society. This has proved to be an endless struggle, requiring effort on at least three fronts: recognition that the problem of unethical and fraudulent behavior is a real one and needs to be countered; building and maintaining a common understanding that countering fraud is everyone's business, public and professionals alike; and the careful crafting of policies and procedures so that incentives for wrongdoing are minimized.

NOTES

1. Lee Porter, *Degrees for Sale* (New York: Arco Publishing Company, 1972), 6.
2. David Brokensha, personal communication, 1 March 2000.
3. David Abel, "Peek Performance: Does the Internet Create More Cheaters, or More Skillful Ones?" *Boston Globe,* 19 March 2000: C1, C5.
4. Kenneth R. Weiss, "New Test-Taking Skill: Working the System," *Los Angeles Times,* 9 January 2000, Internet.
5. Yojana Sharma, "No Thanks for the Memories," *Times Educational Supplement,* 13 September 1996, Internet.
6. George W. S. Trow, "The Harvard Black Rock Forest," *New Yorker,* 11 June 1984: 44–99.
7. "Too Many Teachers Fail, and So Test Is Regraded," *New York Times,* 28 June 1998, Internet.
8. Steven E. Landsburg's "Why Grade Inflation Is Bad for Schools— and What to Do about It" *Slate,* 11 August 1999, Internet, provides an economic analysis of who gains and who loses when grade inflation becomes entrenched in an educational system.
9. Sarah Boseley, "Independent Body Needed to Curb Fraudulent Research," *Guardian Weekly,* 16–22 September 1999: 8.
10. Dirk Johnson, "Cheaters' Final Response: So What?" *New York Times,* 16 May 2000: A16.
11. John Locke, *Some Thoughts Concerning Education* (Indianapolis: Hackett Publishing, 1996), sect. 64.

Index

Abel, David, 143n3
Abitur, 28; due process in, ix
academic honors: countering via
    sanctions, 139–40; four
    approaches to countering,
    136–41; making it unacceptable,
    140–41; reducing incentives,
    136–37; reducing opportunities,
    137–38. *See also* fraud, academic
    honors
Academic Term Papers, 30
accreditation: captive organizations,
    72; false claims, 81
Adler, Larry, 49
Advanced Placement Test, 27
Advertising Council, 54
Agency for International
    Development (AID), 20
Almond, Elliot, 57n42
American Association of
    Collegiate Registrars and
    Admissions Officers
    (AACRAO), 85
American College Test, 27
American Economic Association, 20
American International University,
    70

American Psychological
    Association, Edward Lee
    Thorndike Award, 113
American Society for Clinical
    Oncology, 115
American State University, 70
American Way, 67
American World University
    International, 73
Amupadhi, Joshua, 57n38
Anderton, John, 114
Annals of Internal Medicine, 118
A. R. Baron & Co., 2
Argentina, University of Buenos
    Aires, 65
Arizona, 95
Atlantic Monthly Press, 109
auction houses and fraud, 3–4
Ault, Leslie, 58n60
Austin, Texas, 101
Australia, 33, 35
Austria, 110

baccalauréat, 28, 45; due process
    in, ix
Baluchistan, 37
Bangladesh, 37, 48

About the Authors

Harold J. Noah is Gardner Cowles Professor Emeritus of Economics and Education, Teachers College, Columbia University. He was dean of Teachers College from 1976–1981. For many years he was a member of the faculty of Columbia University's School of International and Public Affairs. He retired from Teachers College in 1987 and joined the faculty of the University at Buffalo, State University of New York, retiring in 1991. Born and educated in London (London School of Economics, and King's College) he has worked in the economics of education and in comparative education. He has been a consultant to OECD, UNESCO, and the World Bank. He is an Honorary Fellow of the Comparative and International Education Society (president from 1973–1974) and a member of the National Academy of Education. He edited the *Comparative Education Review* from 1965 to 1971.

Max A. Eckstein is professor emeritus of Queens College, CUNY and senior research associate, Institute of Philosophy and Politics of Education, Teachers College, Columbia University. Born and educated in England, he received his first degree (B.A.Hons) and professional teaching qualification (P.G.C.E.) at King's College, University of London (1948–1952), and taught English, French, and German in London secondary schools (1952–1957). After joining the faculty of Queens College, CUNY (1958), he obtained the Ph.D. from Teachers College, Columbia University (1964), specializing in comparative education. Former President and now

Honorary Fellow of the Comparative and International Education Society, he has conducted research and lectured in many countries in Asia and Europe. He has served as a consultant on foreign education to the U.S. Department of Education and the American Federation of Teachers.

In addition to their individual books and articles, the authors have co-authored several professional publications, including *Toward a Science of Comparative Education* (1969); *The National Case Study: An Empirical Comparative Study of Twenty-one Educational Systems* (1976); *Secondary School Examinations: International Perspectives on Policies and Practice* (1993); and *Doing Comparative Education: Three Decades of Collaboration* (1998).